HELP YOURSELF TO A JOB

help yourself to a job

a guide for retirees

DOROTHY WINTER

Beacon Press : Boston

Copyright © 1976 by Dorothy Winter

Beacon Press books are published under the auspices of the Unitarian Universalist Association

Published simultaneously in Canada by Fitzhenry & Whiteside, Ltd., Toronto

All rights reserved

Published simultaneously in hardcover and paperback editions

Printed in the United States of America

(hardcover)   9   8   7   6   5   4   3   2   1
(paperback)   9   8   7   6   5   4   3   2   1

Library of Congress Cataloging in Publication Data

Winter, Dorothy.
   Help yourself to a job.
   Includes index.
   1. Age and employment — United States.   I. Title.
HD6280.W55   650'.14   76-7749
ISBN 0-8070-2754-5
ISBN 0-8070-2755-3 (pbk.)

To my sister Jeanette
for her encouragement

CONTENTS

Foreword ix

Chapter 1 **Making the Decision to Return to Work** 1

Why work—Aging myths—How will you perform on the job—What employers look for—Social Security rules—Eligibility for unemployment insurance—Minimum wage law—Age Discrimination in Employment Act.

Chapter 2 **Which Job Is Right for You** 23

Your former occupation—Using skills in a new way—Jobs for the unskilled or semi-skilled—Special problems of women—Analyze your background—Need for more education—Educational programs available.

Chapter 3 **Getting Help from the Government** 38

ACTION programs: Foster Grandparent; Senior Companion—Department of Labor programs: Green Thumb; Green Light; Senior Aides; Senior Community Service Project—Emergency employment—Legislative intern—Retired military—Local programs—Civil service employment.

Chapter 4 **Getting Help from Employment Services** 50

U.S. and State employment service—Commercial employment agencies—Employment services for the elderly—Non-profit senior citizen employment services:

viii   [Help Yourself to a Job

How they operate; Kinds of jobs handled; Other services performed.

Chapter 5   **Finding Work on Your Own**   63

Where to Look—Using want-ads effectively—Phone technique—Letters of application—The interview: Handling the question of age; Other tough questions—Follow-up—Preparing your résumé; Samples.

Chapter 6   **Good Leads for Hard Times**   87

Recession businesses—Job skills needed—Part-time work—Firms that hire the elderly—Selling occupations—Professional fields: Teaching; Consulting work—Sheltered workshops—Skilled trades—Hire yourself: Franchise operation; Cottage industry; Mail-order businesses.

Chapter 7   **Look to the Future**   116

Senior power—Groups working for the elderly—Organize for action—Increase employment opportunities: Expanded labor market; Equal opportunity for jobs; Compensate employers for increased costs; Social Security reform; Extend and enforce the Age Discrimination in Employment Act (ADEA); Case against mandatory retirement.

Appendix A   **State Offices on the Aging**   145

Appendix B **Senior Citizen Employment Services**   149

Index   155

FOREWORD

My father was from the "old school." His work meant everything to him. It nurtured his ego; it sustained his health; it provided him with friends and, of course, a livelihood. To be out of work meant not to be doing anything useful and it was to him the greatest tragedy. When he reached the age of 70, he was not rehired by his employer after a seasonal layoff and he was unable to find another job. It was clear he would never work again, and I was heartsick to see the agony this caused him.

At that time I was unable to help him and I could find no one who would. Since then I have learned much. I have put it in this book in the hope that it will prove helpful to others who want very much to continue to be gainfully employed even though they have reached the age of 60, 70, even 80, or older.

HELP YOURSELF TO A JOB

1

MAKING THE DECISION TO RETURN TO WORK

One of the first things many Americans do today when they retire is to start looking for another job. From all parts of the country come reports that more and more retirees are applying for work—and getting it. Social Security Administration records show that nearly half of the couples registered have at least one member who does some paid work. In fact, close to one-fourth of all men over 65 are in the labor force, including several who are—would you believe—over 100. Employment is so widespread among retirees that income from work accounts for as much as 30 percent of their total income as a group.

WHY WORK?

Financial Need. Why are so many retirees returning to work? A study which asked this question reports that over three-fourths work for financial reasons, the remainder for personal or other reasons. The vast majority work because they have to. The financial bind that so many retirees experience is primarily the result of the convergence of two factors, inflation and the ever-increasing standard of living in America. Inflation, which was of little concern in earlier days, is now so severe and persistent that a retiree trying to make out on a fixed income feels the pressure.

Those of us who were carefully squirreling away a precious few dollars during our middle years occasionally enjoyed the diversion of calculating and recalculating our future pension and retirement income. At the time it appeared quite adequate. We looked forward to the day when lessened family responsibilities would permit us to throw off the restraints and pressures of work and promised ourselves endless days of fishing, or travel, or the like. To our great dismay, however, when the retirement years arrive, the picture has changed. We find that in terms of dollars and cents we just cannot afford to retire.

Yet many are forced to retire by mandatory company policies. Some others retire voluntarily with high hopes, ignoring the cold facts. But as a recent Harris poll reported, a sizable number find retirement not at all what they expected. While the interviewees found their idleness disagreeable, it was primarily financial problems that brought about their discontent. Even as far back as 1680, Saint Evremond wrote, "Nothing is more usual than the sight of an older person who yearns for retirement, and nothing is so rare than those who have retired and do not regret it."

How much money does one need to live in retirement? Arthur Levitt, Comptroller of the State of New York, estimated that 75 percent of one's pre-retirement income is needed to maintain one's previous standard of living. But this is only an approximation, an estimate which does not take into account individual health status, where one lives in retirement, unforeseen emergency needs, and, of course, inflation. Yet economists tell us inflation is now a fact of life and we must accommodate to it. They warn us to look beyond the first year of retirement and to estimate what those future needs may be. Since today a man of 65 can look forward to approximately 13.4 more years of life and a woman to 17.5, a pension check which at first may look quite substantial quickly becomes totally inadequate as inflation increases prices 6, 8, or 10 percent each year of retirement. In 1974 alone prices jumped over 12 percent.

To ignore such future planning can have serious consequences. Unfortunately, many elderly who had never been poor become so in their retirement years; poverty is the plight of all too many of our senior citizens. Figures show that while older Americans represent 10 percent of the population, they account for 20 percent of the poor. In other words, the elderly are disproportionately represented at the poverty level compared to younger persons. The overwhelming majority of the elderly live on less—often much less—than half their former incomes. In 1973 the median income of all families in the United States—the amount above and below which one-half of the families fall—was $12,051. For families headed by an elderly person, the median was about half that amount, or $6,426. Furthermore, about one of every four older families had incomes between $3,000 and $5,000. Older widows and widowers living alone had incomes considerably less. About two-fifths of them lived on less than $2,500 in 1973.

These low retirement incomes appear to reflect the fact that many elderly rely on Social Security for their sole or primary support, although it was never intended for that purpose. It was designed as a base on which to build and not to be the total retirement income itself. Even with the frequent raises in recent years, Social Security alone can provide only a subsistence level of living. Supplemental sources of support are needed to raise the older person above this minimal level. These other sources are most commonly savings, private pensions, and employment.

Savings are not the answer for most people, because only a rare individual can accumulate enough money to matter. The subject of saving money is often the butt of humorists, as in the anecdote about an employer who, congratulating his clerk on his retirement, observed, "So you have $50,000 on which to retire. That shows character and industry." "Yes," replied the man, "I owe it in great part to my abstemious and thrifty habits. Even more I owe it to the carefulness and good management of my good wife. But still more I owe it to the fact that a month ago my aunt died and left me $49,750."

Pensions also most often prove inadequate. You may be surprised to learn that among older retired military officers, half receive less than $4,000 a year, putting them below the national poverty level of $5,600. In reviewing a great number of pension plans we found that only a handful of those negotiated by unions are designed to keep pace with the cost of living, and none make provision for increases in standard of living. Yet in American society the standard of living is constantly on the rise. You see it clearly when you realize that such items as air conditioning, private automobiles, weekend and vacation trips, rarities in our younger days, are now considered necessities by most people. Older persons who cannot afford to keep up with changes in life style find themselves out of the mainstream of life. Older persons, no less than younger ones, want to enjoy the good life, and so they continue to consume in retirement at the same level as before. Experience has not borne out the long-held belief that older people need less money.

It comes down to one important fact. For a challenging, rewarding, and comfortable retirement, you need adequate income—an income which not only can keep pace with inflation but, equally important, with our increasing standard of living. The answer for many retirees is continued employment. The prospect of a regular pay check at today's higher wage scale motivates many elderly to return to work. Mark Twain once remarked, "Virtue has never been as respectable as money."

Psychological and Social Reasons. Some people have reasons other than financial for working. Many see post-retirement employment as an opportunity to continue to use skills and knowledge developed over a lifetime of living. The sense of continued usefulness and the feeling of accomplishment adds meaning to their lives. The intellectual stimulation and sense of identity that work provides are hard to replace with leisure-time activities. Certainly the arts and crafts and socializing of organized senior citizen clubs falls short of filling the gap for most elderly.

Many find only boredom in retirement. The novelty of sleeping late soon wears off and one quickly runs out of friends and relatives to visit. Four or five times a week of golf soon tapers off to once a week. A fishing schedule of twice a week becomes a once-a-week affair and then stretches into a now-and-then occasion. Free time begins to hang heavy. Boredom sets in and often pushes older people into isolation, with its very serious consequences. Returning to work, however, offers the prospect of new social contacts and the moral support that only other people can provide. On the job, unlike in any other situation, one can observe how others cope with life's challenges. Psychologists see such contacts as having a stabilizing effect on older persons who, when isolated, have a tendency to exaggerate their personal problems. Doctors warn that many physical ailments actually result from inactivity, loneliness, and depression. In such an atmosphere, symptoms of illness accelerate and appetite, digestion, sleep, and cardiovascular function suffer.

Of course we must acknowledge that work almost always has a double aspect. Often it is bondage or wearisome drudgery, but it is also a source of interest, a steadying element, and the factor that helps integrate an individual with society. Ours is still a work-oriented society which segregates us not so much by age as by our productivity. The retiree who chooses to work even a few hours a week usually enjoys greater personal and family esteem. A 70-year-old woman who took a job as a relief telephone operator told me, "You just can't imagine until it happens to you, the feeling you have when you receive that first pay check. It's as if the world is telling you that they still need and want you, and that's really wonderful to know." Another elderly lady put it this way: "I still have plenty of good years ahead. Retirement is like cutting down a tree. I like my work. Here I feel like somebody, but at home I'm nobody." The same reaction was found in a study that compared a large number of retired with non-retired persons over the age of 65. The researchers learned that general satisfaction with life was significantly lower in the retired group.

Many people find that work gives a regularity to their lives; a basic rhythm and pattern of day, week, month, and year. Without work, time patterns become confused. Picasso remarked, "Work is another way of keeping a diary." I also remember the words of a stately old gentleman who pleaded with me to help him find employment. Having worked hard all his life making milk deliveries in the wee hours of every morning, he was now retired all of two weeks. "When my feet hit the ground in the morning," he said, "I must know they have somewhere to go."

For a Longer Life. Studies seem to point to work satisfaction as the best predictor of longevity. While other factors are known to be important in extending life—diet, exercise, medical care, and genetic inheritance—the work role and work conditions have been found to contribute significantly. Doctors, observing that work helps the vital organs function optimally, point out that some measure of occupational activity, adapted to the physical and mental capabilities of the retired person, is one of the best methods of slowing down the aging process. The Veterans Administration in their "Normative Aging Study" supported this idea. The study predicts that if we were to increase the age of retirement to 100, it would lead to a normal life expectancy of 120 to 140 years. In the words of the report, "the utility ceiling set by a given culture determines the age of death. If an older individual has a need for the years beyond 70, he will retain competence and live longer."

Today in societies where people live to a very old age, no one retires. The elderly continue to do strenuous work. In Abkhasia in the republic of Georgia in the U.S.S.R., persons of 100 or more are reported to be doing physical labor. Currently, two other communities besides Abkhasia are receiving a lot of attention because Methuselah-like ages as high as 130 and 140 are not uncommon. These areas are located in widely separated parts of the world. Vilcabamba is a small village tucked into a lush valley in the Andes of Ecuador, and Hunza is located in the mountainous part of the Pakistani Kashmir. Investigators seeking to at least partially explain these long-lived communities have found some interesting similarities among them. In all three places the aged are esteemed and almost envied for their years, which are believed to bring them wisdom. Also in all three there is a very high level of physical activity for people of all ages. Rocking chairs are nonexistent. Men in their 90s put in a full day's work in the fields and women of close to 100 are still involved in community activities and household chores.

AGING MYTHS

Although predictions of longer life, added income, and psychological and social advantages are reason enough, the decision to return to work is not easy for most people. As a retiree, you may wonder whether you will have the ability to hold down a new job after having been on the same one for 10, 20, perhaps 40 years. You are probably vague about the kind of job you want. You question what types of positions are available, and in fact whether any jobs are open to men and women of your age. If these are your thoughts, be assured that many other retirees share them.

Most of your questions will be answered in subsequent chapters, but here I want to deal with the ability of older people to work. For most people, 65 is not really old anymore. A man or woman of 65 today is biologically as young as a person of 40 to 45 in 1900. True, there is a higher incidence of illness in old age, but it is not a necessary accompaniment of aging. The findings of a recent Gallup poll are that 60 percent of those over 60 can do almost anything they want to do. For persons over 65, a National Health Survey found that at least half are in sufficiently good health to work. Between the ages of 65 and 74, over one-fourth of the men and over one-fifth of the women suffer no chronic condition. An additional one-third have one or more chronic ailments but no limitation of activity. For those aged 75 and over, 45 percent have no limitation of activity.

Many of the myths of aging have been debunked by studies conducted under the Older Americans Act passed by Congress in 1965. Research findings have destroyed the long-accepted notion that mental deterioration is inevitable with age. This myth is so prevalent that many elderly come to believe it of themselves. For example, does a temporary loss of memory drive you into a minor panic, with the fear that senility is setting in? If you worry about it and become depressed, you will indeed suffer physically. But loss of memory can occur at any age, and the elderly are no more subject to this phenomenon than any other age group. As for senility, it just is not an inevitable part of aging. Dr. James

Birren, renowned gerontologist who conducts experimental research at the Ethel Percy Andrus Gerontological Center of the University of Southern California, tells us that only about 12 percent of the population have the genetic predisposition for the brain disorder that causes senility, and of those, only 5 percent eventually develop it. Researchers have suggested that the quickest cure for senility might be to abandon the word.

Compulsory retirement is to some extent based on the belief that everybody eventually loses his thinking capacity. A person's I.Q. was thought to rise through youth and adolescence, reach a plateau in the 30s, and slowly but surely decline after 40. Evidence is now available that shows that once intelligence has reached its peak, it stays at that level into old age, but only if one remains active and continues to use one's mind. Both the mind and the body will deteriorate with lack of activity and exercise. The mind needs exposure to new learning experiences. Those elderly who withdraw from regular activity, often because of retirement and the lack of any definite function in our society, do suffer physical and mental deterioration. Physiologists have shown that even young persons put on extended bed rest, or placed in confining plaster casts, or immersed in water for long periods of time, begin to show the physiological deterioration typically associated with rapid aging.

HOW WILL YOU PERFORM ON THE JOB?

Experimental findings show chronological age to be a poor determinant of a person's intelligence and work performance. In one study, healthy people over 70 scored higher than younger persons on tests of arithmetic operation, vocabulary, and comprehension of verbal statements. In fact, as we grow into our senior years, our ability to store large amounts of information appears to improve. However, the older person's performance tends to decline on tests that emphasize speed, since younger people are able to respond more quickly. But on the job older persons make up for this deficiency in the high quality of their work and the consistency of their performance.

Not only are the elderly able to produce a volume of work equal to that put out by younger employees but in some circumstances they even outproduce them. This was brought out in a recent survey of state agencies undertaken by the Commission on Human Rights of the State of New York to ascertain the work performance of persons over 65. All agencies in the study rated the employees over 65 high on performance, with 88 percent reporting their performance "about equal to" and 12 percent "noticeably better than" that of workers under 65. Of the agencies surveyed, 64 percent indicated that employees over 65 were generally as punctual as those under 65, and some even reported noticeably more punctuality among the older workers, with no agency reporting less. Employees over 65 had equal or better safety records than younger employees. There appeared to be no special problems in the continued employment of persons over 65, and in only one instance was it mentioned that employees in this age group are generally unable to perform the more physically demanding jobs.

Even when it comes to strenuous physical activity there are numerous examples of older persons which refute the latter statement. We often read of famous personalities who continue to perform actively and well in their later years. Karl Wallenda, the famous tightrope walker, is 68. Hazel Hotchkiss at 74 was still competing in tennis matches. Artur Rubinstein at 89 played a note-perfect performance with such spirit, ardor, and power that he brought down the house. Sally Rand, 70 and a grandmother, is still strutting her stuff and doing her famous fan dance on a 40-week-a-year tour schedule. When asked why she did not just do a couple of weeks in Las Vegas each year, she replied, "This is a physical thing. If I don't do it every day, then I can't do it at all. During idle periods I take ballet classes every day at my home." An Oklahoma woman of 88 who walks a 10-mile paper route daily to service almost 200 customers commented, "If older people don't do something, they start to rust, and they wind up sitting in wheelchairs."

Have you heard about the Senior Olympics? Held mostly in the area around Los Angeles, California, it is a series of athletic events which have absolutely no top age limit. The competitions range from archery and basketball to water polo and wrestling. Among the geri-athletes is a 70-year-old who ran 1,500 meters in 5:30.8, a 75-year-old who won two tennis titles in 100-degree heat, and another man of 75 who competed in 16 events in 3 different sports. The competition uses the slogan "Youth Eternal." On the East Coast, in St. Petersburg, Florida, there is the Three-Quarter-Century Softball Club. Composed of members all over the age of 75, the club's two teams play each other every week from November to March. Hitting line drives, running around bases, and doing expert outfielding is an 88-year-old man. The catcher, who is 91, plays with a bad back; another player has a pacemaker in his heart. But all say they play "to live."

Now look at some other people who have worked into their old old age:

Michelangelo was sculpturing until a few weeks before his death in his 90th year.

Titian was still painting at 99.

Sol Hurok at 85 looked back on 60 years as an entertainment impresario. He is said to have had an obsessive determination never to retire.

Charlie Smith, reported to be the oldest man in the United States, is 132 and still runs a candy and soft drink store in Bartow, Florida. He likes to tell of the day in 1955 when the boss of the citrus grove where he worked climbing trees told him to retire. He was then 113 years of age.

Lowell Thomas, 82, was still on the air signing off his newscast with the familiar, "so long, until tomorrow."

At 79, Jimmy Durante was growling out, "Inka Dinka Doo" and "Who Will Be With You When I'm Far Away?" Asked when he would retire, he replied, "Retire for what? The minute you quit, you become nothing."

Margaret Mead at 72 edits books, gives lectures, and travels many hundreds of miles a year.

Winston Churchill was a great world leader at 81.

Oliver Wendell Holmes was still on the Supreme Court at 91. In a brief speech he summed up his view of retirement. "The work never is done while the power to work remains . . . to live is to function."

Arturo Toscanini was conducting magnificently at 87.

Connie Mack led the Athletics at 88.

Gayelord Hauser, the famous nutritionist, at 80 has just finished a new cookbook and is off on another of his endless lecture tours.

Dumas Malone won the 1975 Pulitzer Prize in history at 83, and gained the distinction of being the oldest person ever to receive the award.

J. Paul Getty, the 82-year-old billionaire, did not count his billions in solitary splendor but made all the major decisions for the oil company that bears his name.

John Houseman at 71 recently won an Academy Award for his supporting role in the movie *The Paper Chase*. To the suggestion that he may be nearing retirement, he replied, "Hell, no!"

George Burns at 78 just finished a one-man show in Los Angeles.

Lawrence Welk at 71 looks like a man in his 50s and shows no signs of laying down his baton.

Nor does Guy Lombardo, who at 72 performs 48 weeks out of the year, plus New Year's Eve. He has no thought of retiring. "I don't even like the sound of the word," he says. "I don't feel any different now than I did at 30. Not a bit."

George Meany at 81 is still Mr. Labor, ruling over the federation of 14 million trade unionists, the A.F.L.–C.I.O.

Irving Stone, 72, writer of best sellers starting with *Lust for Life* in 1934, has just received a new contract from his publisher for three more novels. At his estimated writing time of 5 years for each, that means approximately 15 years of future endeavor.

Jean Renoir, frequently called the father of the French film, recently turned 80 and finished another movie. He remarked, "This, I believe, is one recipe for happiness: to work with people you love and who love you. The advantage of being 80 years old is that one has had many people to love."

If you think famous personalities are somehow different from ordinary people, please note the following:

A doctor in Elizabethtown, Kentucky, is still working at 96. He says simply, "I just got in the habit, and I can't quit."

Ralph D. of Nyack, New York, has been working steadily for 63 of his 82 years. Now a personal secretary to a wealthy personage, he remarks, "That's why I'm alive today, because I'm still working."

Will S. of Franklin, Nebraska, like so many other farmers is still tending his cattle at 72. His wife says, "Farming isn't work. It's a way of life. Now, how can you retire from a way of life?"

Mel H. is 82 and slowing down somewhat. He sold his farm implement dealership and now only cares for 100 cattle and 1,640 acres of land.

Joseph D. at 75 handles a demanding job as superintendent of highways for a small town in New York. He loves his work and hopes he will never have to retire. "I'll work until the man upstairs says I can't."

Roy B. is still barbering at 97 in Albany, Wisconsin.

John W., a grocer in East Orange, New Jersey, celebrated his 100th birthday. "Nobody ever died from hard work," he says.

WHAT EMPLOYERS LOOK FOR

Evidence like the foregoing is helping to change attitudes toward the older worker. There is growing recognition of the older person's wish to work and his ability to do so. Employers are taking a second look and becoming aware that it is not reasonable to assume that a man who was a valuable member of the work force at 64½ is too old to hire at 65.

Employers of older workers have been questioned about what attributes influenced their willingness to employ the elderly. Experience rated first, then stability, dependability, and knowledge. Next came good work habits, attitude, pride in work, consistent performance, sound judgment, less supervision needed, loyalty, and less job hopping. One hotel owner in the Midwest was so impressed with the patience of older persons that he employed only senior citizens in areas having a contact with the public. He felt they were able to create the warmth of atmosphere he wanted.

Here are direct quotes from other employers:

Florist: "Charlie retired from his former profession four years ago, but couldn't stand the leisure life, so he came to drive for us, delivering flowers and plants. He loves his job and says he wants to continue with us for a long time. We're thrilled because we think he's the greatest."

Resort hotel and restaurant manager: "Older persons generally want jobs that do not demand much lifting and stair-climbing. But don't let that fool you. They are willing to work hard, very hard, often because they either need the money badly or really enjoy working. More elderly are ready to accept responsibilities as compared to kids, who just want to make a few bucks so they can disappear the next good beach day."

Motel owner: "We give preference to elderly persons in certain situations—desk clerk, working on the switchboard—because they are more careful about details and more mature, having been in business before."

Fuel oil dealer: "I hired a retired executive as a consultant to help us with management problems. His wisdom and knowledge are extremely valuable. In sales we have older men too. They are very successful in calling on young marrieds. The 'father' image is still a potent factor. Also, in the service department I find that older mechanics, although perhaps not quite as fast as the younger men, generally have better 'call back' records because of their experience and skill in diagnosing problems and their patience in making the repairs. In a seasonal business like retailing of fuel oil, employing the older worker is the answer to our ever-increasing operating costs."

SOCIAL SECURITY RULES

I hope by now your doubts about finding employment are beginning to disappear and that you are thinking seriously about a job. Your first concern probably is the effect it will

14 [Help Yourself to a Job

have on your Social Security payments; that is, how much you may earn without disturbing your monthly checks. For the year 1976, the answer is $2,760. Over that amount your wages will trigger a reduction in your Social Security check. The $2,760 maximum, often called the "retirement test," is subject to change periodically, so look for increases in the future. During the recent past it has been raised annually by Congressional action but it will now go up automatically as the level of average earnings in the labor market increases.

If you earn over the $2,760 maximum during the calendar year of 1976, you will lose $1 in Social Security payments for every additional $2 of wages. For example: Suppose your benefit rate is $275 a month and you earn $400 each month on your job for a total of $4,800 for the year. Since $2,040 of your earnings is in excess of the $2,760 limit ($4,800 − $2,760 = $2,040), the rule of losing $1 for each $2 of earnings applies to this amount. Your loss in social security benefits is half that amount, or $1,020. With the $2,280 that you would still receive from Social Security plus the $4,800 in earnings, your total income would be $7,080 for the year. The table on page 15 will give you other examples.

Each person in a family getting benefits can have earnings within the prescribed limit. For example, a retired husband and his wife may each earn $2,760 and suffer no reduction in benefits. However, if the retired worker has earnings over the limit, the excess earnings are charged against the total family benefits payable on his or her account. Thus a retired worker's earnings might reduce his dependents' benefits, but a dependent's excess earnings will reduce only his or her own benefits.

Exceptions to the Retirement Test. There are two exceptions which allow you to keep more of your Social Security benefit. One exception applies to monthly earnings, the other only to persons 72 or older. The monthly rule permits you, no matter how high your earnings are for the year, to receive your full Social Security benefit for any month in which you earn $230 or less and do not perform substantial services in self-

Amount of Social Security Payment You Keep if Your Earnings Are Over $2,760 for the Year

Monthly Benefit	Total Earnings (in shaded blocks)							
	$2,760	$3,000	$3,500	$4,000	$5,000	$6,000	$7,000	$8,000
$ 75	900	780	530	280	0	0	0	0
100	1,200	1,080	830	580	80	0	0	0
125	1,500	1,380	1,130	880	380	0	0	0
150	1,800	1,680	1,430	1,180	680	180	0	0
175	2,100	1,980	1,730	1,480	980	480	0	0
200	2,400	2,280	2,030	1,780	1,280	780	280	0
225	2,700	2,580	2,330	2,080	1,580	1,080	580	80
250	3,000	2,880	2,630	2,380	1,880	1,380	880	380
275	3,300	3,180	2,930	2,680	2,180	1,680	1,180	680
300	3,600	3,480	3,230	2,980	2,480	1,980	1,480	980
325	3,900	3,780	3,530	3,280	2,780	2,280	1,780	1,280
350	4,200	4,080	3,830	3,580	3,080	2,580	2,080	1,580
400	4,800	4,680	4,430	4,180	3,680	3,180	2,680	2,180
450	5,400	5,280	5,030	4,780	4,280	3,780	3,280	2,780
500	6,000	5,880	5,630	5,380	4,880	4,380	3,880	3,380
550	6,600	6,480	6,230	5,980	5,480	4,980	4,480	3,980

employment. What constitutes "performing substantial services" will be explained later. Here I want to explain how the monthly rule works if your earnings are from wages only. For example, if you should work during the summer months, say May through September, and even if you earn as much as $8,000 during these months, you will receive your full social security benefits for the remaining months, January through April and October through December. You receive full payments for the seven months in which you did no work. Then, if your monthly Social Security check is, for example, $275, you would still receive $1,925 ($275 for seven months = $1,925) even though you would receive no Social Security for the months May through September (five months). Your total income would be the $8,000 you earned during the summer plus the $1,925 Social Security, for a total of $9,925 for the year. Retirees who do consulting work often take advantage of this rule. They arrange to perform their services at a high fee for a few months a year and still continue to receive their Social Security for the other months in which they did not earn more than $230. The $230 monthly limit applies only during 1976 and is subject to change each time the annual retirement test figure of $2,760 is revised.

The second exception to the retirement test rule applies to persons 72 or older. When you reach that age, there are no restrictions on the amount of money you may earn. The sky's the limit. No matter how high your earnings after 72, there will be no reduction in your Social Security payments. For an explanation of the method used to determine the maximum earnings allowed in the calendar year in which you turn 72, contact your Social Security office. In fact, it is important that all persons of 65, whether or not they are still employed, get in touch with their Social Security office. This will insure that you do not lose any benefits to which you may be entitled. For example, anyone who is eligible for Social Security automatically qualifies for Medicare payments.

Which Earnings Count. Total wages before deductions, not just take-home pay, are used for Social Security purposes. You must count earnings from work of any kind, whether or not it is covered by Social Security. However, tips amounting to less than $20 a month are excluded. Domestic employees and farm workers need only include cash wages, not meals or living quarters which may be provided by the employer. Income not earned on a job or in self-employment does not count. Thus, income from savings, investments, pensions, insurance, royalties, or rent will not affect your Social Security checks.

A self-employed person need only count as income his net profit (after allowable business expenses) from any enterprise in which he is sole owner or partner. Fees paid you as a director of a corporation are considered earnings from self-employment. If you have earnings from both wages and self-employment, they are added together.

For self-employed persons the rule requires withholding benefits in any month in which you perform substantial services in a trade or business. There is no fixed definition of what constitutes "performing substantial services," but the time you devote to your business, the kind of services you perform, and how your services compare with those you performed in past years are all taken into consideration. Generally, if you work more than 45 hours a month at your trade or business, it will be considered substantial. For some highly skilled occupations or sizable businesses, as few as 20 hours have been used as the measure. However, if you work fewer than 15 hours in a month, your services are not considered substantial, regardless of the size of the business or the value of the service. The time counted includes all time spent planning or managing the business, even if it is done away from the place of business.

Reporting Your Income to Social Security. When you return to work after starting to receive your Social Security checks and you expect your annual earnings to be more than $2,760 (1976), you should notify your Social Security office. The method they use for adjusting your benefits is as follows: Each year you will be asked to estimate the amount you expect to earn in the coming year. Then the benefits you receive in that year will be based on your estimate. If you overestimate your expected earnings, you will receive a check for the unpaid amount when you report your actual earnings at the end of the year. If your estimate is under what you actually earned, when you report at the end of the year, you will be required to pay back the excess or have it withheld from your checks in the following year.

How Working Increases Your Social Security. Should you delay your retirement until after 65 and not start collecting any of your checks, you will receive a special credit that could mean a larger Social Security check in the future. Between your 65th and 72nd birthdays, for each year in which you forego your Social Security checks because you are working, you will receive a credit of one percent ($\frac{1}{12}$ of one percent for each month). This credit will be added to your checks when you decide to take them. The increase, however, applies only to your own checks, not those of your dependents or survivors.

If you return to work after starting to receive your Social Security checks, you will continue to pay into the Social Security fund through the usual payroll deductions if you earn $50 or more in a calendar quarter, for most work, or $400 or more per year from self-employment. These new payments will also result in higher benefits to you in the future. The Social Security Administration will automatically refigure your benefit whenever additional earnings are credited to your record.

Effect on Supplementary Security Payments. For individuals with very low incomes who receive supplementary security income assistance, working part-time may affect these payments. The rule is that the first $65 earned each month will be exempt in calculating your income, but half of the remainder of your earnings will be counted to reduce the amount you receive in supplementary payments.

ELIGIBILITY FOR UNEMPLOYMENT INSURANCE

Individuals who return to work after retirement may be eligible for unemployment insurance benefits during their job search. You may be eligible for such payments even while collecting your Social Security checks. The determination is usually based on whether you were compulsorily retired by your employer. To give you an idea of how this works, following are the general rules that apply in New York, New Jersey, and Connecticut. Check your state office for unemployment compensation for the rules in your state.

In New York, a person who leaves his job because of corporate policies on mandatory retirement may be considered eligible for unemployment insurance benefits, but those who retire voluntarily are said to apply for such benefits "without good cause" and are not eligible. Of course the person who has been required to retire must convince the state Labor Department that he is willing and able to work in order to collect unemployment benefits.

In New Jersey, a person who is ordered to retire may collect unemployment insurance benefits if he meets all other eligibility requirements, such as number of weeks worked and total earnings in the previous year. If an individual retires voluntarily in New Jersey, he is still eligible for unemployment insurance benefits under certain conditions. For instance, he could collect benefits if he obtained a new job after retirement and after a minimum period of time is subsequently discharged.

In Connecticut, those forced to retire are also eligible for unemployment insurance benefits as long as they are considered active members of the labor force. There are also some circumstances that permit those who retire voluntarily to qualify for unemployment benefits. An example is a person who retired from a particular job for health reasons but who might be able to accept another type of position if it were available. In Connecticut, however, unemployment benefits could be reduced by the amount of a company pension.

MINIMUM WAGE LAW

Two other laws that will affect you should you return to work are the minimum wage law and the Age Discrimination in Employment Act, for each of which there are federal regulations and some state laws. Where there are differences in the state and federal laws, the higher standard applies.

Regarding the minimum wage law, there are unfortunately many employers who disregard its provisions for they believe that older people are willing to work for nothing or for a pittance, just to keep busy. Some employers believe the myth that Social Security payments make older people financially secure. This problem is often compounded by retirees who wish to keep their earnings under the Social Security limit and therefore accept less than the going wage, or work longer hours than they are paid for. I caution older people not to permit themselves to be exploited in this way. Whoever contributes work to a profit-making enterprise is entitled to a fair wage. Knowing the law will help you to protect yourself.

The federal minimum wage law passed in 1974 requires employers to pay at least $2.30 an hour beginning in 1976 to all non-agricultural workers previously covered. For newly covered employees (that is, those brought under the law by 1966 and later amendments), the minimum wage for 1976 is $2.20, with an increase to $2.30 an hour in 1977. Newly covered workers are domestic help, such as housekeepers, cooks, and chauffeurs who receive at least $50 in cash wages in any calendar quarter or work more than 8 hours a week. Government workers, motion picture theater employees, and small crews of loggers also come under the federal regulations now. However, persons employed as casual baby sitters or home companions to the disabled or elderly are still not included in the minimum wage law.

Agricultural workers are now entitled to a minimum wage of $2.00 an hour, with increases to $2.20 an hour in 1977, and $2.30 an hour in 1978. Only farmers who use more than 500 man-days of labor in a three-month period are required to pay the minimum wage.

Some exceptions are also made for employers of non-agricultural employees. For example, certain small retail or service establishments that make most of their sales within the state are exempt. Hospitals, nursing homes, laundries, dry cleaners, and schools, however, do not qualify for this exemption. This provision is due to be phased out and ultimately repealed on January 1, 1977, for chain stores in a covered enterprise. Certain seasonal amusement or recreational establishments as well as small newspapers and fishing operations are not covered by the law. Executive, administrative, and professional employees (including teachers and academic administrative personnel in schools), and outside salesworkers are also exempted. All in all, the federal law now protects about two-thirds of the labor force. If you wish to check on any exceptions to the law or the rate applicable to any specific position, contact your nearest office of the Wage and Hour Division of the Department of Labor. It will be listed under U.S. Government in your phone directory.

Thirty-nine states, the District of Columbia, Guam, and Puerto Rico have minimum wage laws in effect. Some of these state regulations may differ from the federal law. In New York State, the minimum wage now coincides with the federal regulations except for farm workers' coverage. While the federal law applies to about one-fifth of all farm workers, the New York law covers almost all farm workers by excluding only those employers with annual payrolls of less than $1,200. For residents of other states, your state Department of Labor will be able to inform you of any state extensions of the federal rules.

AGE DISCRIMINATION IN EMPLOYMENT ACT

Those retirees over 65 who believe that the federal Age Discrimination in Employment Act (ADEA) prevents employers from discriminating against them are misinformed. The law does prohibit discrimination in matters of hiring, job retention, compensation, and other terms of employment, but the ADEA unfortunately applies *only* to individuals between the ages of 40 and 65. Efforts to remove the upper age limit of 65 from the ADEA have so far been ineffective. For those under 65 the law provides protection if they work for, or apply to, an employer of 20 or more persons. Public and private employment agencies serving employers of 20 or more persons and labor organizations are also subject to the regulations of the ADEA. Federal, state, and local governments are included, although a court challenge has stayed enforcement on public police and fire department employees, pending a Supreme Court ruling.

The Age Discrimination in Employment Act has been on the books since 1968 but many people still know little about it, perhaps because the law has not been widely publicized until recently. The United States Department of Labor's Wage and Hour Division, which is charged with enforcing the ADEA, found on investigation that forty percent of all employers were in violation of it. With limited funds available for enforcement, the Labor Department relies primarily on voluntary compliance by employers. Of the 3,000 complaints reported each year, few are brought to trial. In the last few years, however, there has been more vigorous enforcement and some notable decisions have been made. For example, damages were awarded twenty-eight former employees of a major airline who were laid off, retired, or assigned to inactive status because they were over 59. And an agreement was made by a unit of Standard Oil Company of California to pay $2 million in back wages to 160 employees discharged because of age (which varied from 40 to 65), and to rehire those who had not reached 65 at the time the case was resolved. Pending in the courts is a case against two major railroad companies testing the legality of company pension plans that impose mandatory retirement at age 65 or younger. And the City of New York averted a court case when it heeded the warning of the U.S. Secretary of Labor that its planned forced retirement of all employees 62 or older could be in violation of the law. That a governing body as large as the City of New York could attempt such questionable action adds weight to the importance of individuals knowing the law and how it applies to them.

Some states have broadened the application of the Age Discrimination in Employment Act within their jurisdictions. In New York State, for instance, the state law covers employers of four or more workers (the federal law applies to twenty or more workers). As for the 65 age limit, the following ten states have eliminated the maximum in their state laws: Alaska, Hawaii, Illinois, Iowa, Maine, Maryland, Montana, Nevada, New Jersey, New Mexico, as well as Guam and the Virgin Islands. To determine whether your state has enacted its own age discrimination law and what its terms are, write to the U.S. Department of Labor, Wage and Hour Division, Washington, D.C. 20210, or your state Department of Labor or Commission on Human Rights. These are also the appropriate offices to contact if you feel you are being discriminated against in employment because of your age. In Chapter 7 there is a further discussion of the U.S. Age Discrimination in Employment Act, its shortcomings and possible solutions.

2

WHICH JOB IS RIGHT FOR YOU

YOUR FORMER OCCUPATION

After you have made the decision to return to work, your next thoughts will be on what kind of job to look for. You may wonder whether to stay in your former line of work or search for something new. In this regard, remember that work experience has always been one of the most highly valued attributes in the job market. Because of this, I often advise retirees returning to work to continue in the occupation they pursued in the past. Most older workers do just that. They can usually find work more readily that way and also earn more. Especially for those who have a profession or technical skill, chances of finding work after retirement are best in their own field.

If you can still do your job and if people are being hired in your field, concentrate your efforts in that direction. However, if you can no longer handle your former work, or if you believe that no opportunities exist, examine your other skills and see whether they point to any different jobs. Perhaps you can utilize a hobby or an incidental skill. Have you been doing repairs around the house, home sewing, home decorating, car repairing, gardening, photography? Are these skills now good enough to warrant payment? Many people successfully switch to a different line of work at this stage in life. Such a change was made by a former restaurant owner who had enjoyed collecting antiques as a hobby. He easily found part-time employment with a neighborhood antique store where he acts as a relief sales clerk. A former mortgage broker of 70 who put to use his hobby of singing in the church choir now collects modest fees and enjoys entertaining at senior citizen clubs and day care centers. Another senior citizen who retired after 28 years as an inspector of gyroscopes and other airplane technical devices had always enjoyed repairing his own cars and those of his friends. On his first day of job hunting after retirement, he was hired by a local auto repair service.

USING SKILLS IN A NEW WAY

If you lack a suitable hobby, then consider whether you can utilize your old skill in a new way. For someone with a highly developed or unusual skill, consulting work, teaching, or lecturing might be considered. Perhaps a local school or adult education center can use you, or an appropriate local store. For example, a seamstress could teach at a local fabric store, a musician at a music shop, an artist at an art supply store or art gallery. A teacher could sell books or school equipment, or serve as a consultant. A railroad retiree could be useful as a freight dispatcher for a factory. Here are some examples of individuals who used this approach:

A semi-retired freelance commercial artist of 62 easily found a job selling paintings in an art gallery and uses his free time there to work on his own projects.

Another retired artist was able to find employment teaching an art course at the neighborhood community college.

A former wholesale fur manufacturer uses his knowledge of payroll preparation (an incidental skill in his former occupation) to help a neighborhood camera shop owner and a local restaurateur prepare their payrolls.

A former driver and supervisor for a city bus company bought his own panel truck and handles light delivery jobs with it. Working on a part-time basis, he now enjoys the luxury for the first time in his working life, of adjusting his hours to his own schedule.

Similarly, a man who drove a taxicab for over 23 years now delivers flowers for a local florist.

A highly efficient typist, retired from government service at the early age of 55, established a lucrative business typing manuscripts in her own home at her own pace.

A former marine engineer who handled the ordering of supplies for a shipping line now writes orders and checks supplies for a local building contractor. In addition, he acts as the resident maintenance man in his retirement community, adding to his income the payment he receives on a job-by-job basis.

And a retired nurse who no longer wanted the pressure of hospital routine became a nurse in a summer day camp, a job that permits her to pursue her love of travel during the remainder of the year.

JOBS FOR THE UNSKILLED OR SEMI-SKILLED

If you can't work a similar switch with your experience, or if you simply are tired of your former line of work and want a change, there are certain types of jobs not requiring physical strain or specialized training that you can consider. However, you should be aware that because of their unskilled nature, these jobs usually warrant pay only at the minimum wage level. Following is a list of these jobs which are appropriate for older men and women:

Aide—child care, health, hospital ward, laboratory, library, lunch program, nurse's, school, teacher's, visual equipment, nursery school helper. These jobs are found in schools, day care centers, senior centers, hospitals, and other institutions.

Artist's Model

Attendant, for art galleries, museums, parks, parking lots, playgrounds, service stations.

Babysitter, in homes and child care agencies.

Cafeteria Worker, also coffee shop waitress, kitchen helper, and food server in lunchrooms.

Cashier, also ticket taker, or toll collector; in stores, theaters, parks, on bridges.

Chauffeur, also driver or delivery man for light items, such as flowers or drugs; for businesses or individuals.

Collector, for bills or rent or credit checker.

Companion, to youths and older persons who are homebound or institutionalized; also homemaker or reader to blind or sick people.

Cook

Cottage Parent or House Mother, in institutions, camps, and schools.

Demonstrator, for products or services.

Domestic

Doorman

Elevator Operator

Entertainer, for hospitals, institutions, prisons, senior centers, or schools.

Floorwalker

Gardener, also groundskeeper

General Office Worker, also business machines operator, file clerk, mail handler.

Guard, also watchman and caretaker for banks, factories, hospitals, institutions, museums, or parks.

Handyman, also custodian, janitor, maintenance man and building superintendent in homes, factories, and institutions.

Housesitter, also pet and plant sitter.

Interviewer, also canvasser for surveys, handbill distributing, door-to-door sales.

Light Industrial Worker, assembling electrical components, making candy, packaging small items, operating a sewing machine.

Party Helper, for private homes, institutions, or caterers.

Porter

Printer's Helper, also proofreader

Receptionist, also desk clerk, night attendant; for business offices, professional offices, hospitals, hotels.

Relief personnel, for shopkeepers during lunch or supper hours, or peak hours.

Salesclerk

Salesman, of real estate, wholesale items, or advertising.

School Crossing Guard

Shipping and Receiving Clerk, also packer, wrapper.
Shopper, for comparison shopping services or housebound individuals.
Speaker or Lecturer
Switchboard Operator
Teacher, of skills, crafts, hobbies, or homemaking.
Telephone Solicitor
Teller, also vault custodian in a bank.
Travel Agent
Usher
Waiter or Waitress

Of the above list, clerical work, salesclerking, guard duty, and light industrial work are the most popular with retirees. Retail sales work in particular is one of the easiest jobs for the retiree to obtain. Women are especially wanted in this field, though men are hired to work in areas catering to male customers, such as hardware, sporting goods, lumber yards, and major appliances. In these areas, where the salesman's advice on product performance and maintenance is frequently sought, the older man with experience or specialized knowledge is often a welcome employee. Service sales jobs, such as securities, real estate, insurance, transportation service, are also dominated by men.

Another area using mostly men is guard duty. Lately, security guard companies seem to have an unlimited demand for such help. They look primarily for retirees with police or military training, but even former laborers are readily accepted. Many guard positions, however, require night hours or weekend work. If you are willing to accept these hours, you should have no difficulty finding a job in this field.

If you are inclined towards industrial work, you will find that light manufacturing employs a fair proportion of working retirees. This differs drastically from the manufacturing field as a whole, which hires few older workers. But factories working on small products find that the patience and attention to detail characteristic of many elderly are particularly desirable in their type of work.

SPECIAL PROBLEMS OF WOMEN

Women who have been full-time homemakers and have had little or no employment outside the home are faced with a special problem when they look for work. These mature women feel especially insecure about job hunting. For women who have raised children, one obvious possibility is a nursery or child care agency where they can use their child-rearing skills. The demand for this kind of help appears unlimited, so that any woman who loves children, and vice versa, is assured of never being out of work. Even some women with business experience enjoy this kind of work. A woman "over 65" who had held down a responsible bookkeeping and secretarial position applied for work at an employment service but refused to consider office positions offered her. She preferred the satisfaction of babysitting and got all the work she could handle.

Companion jobs to elderly or invalid adults, or work as aides in hospitals, schools, or institutions are other jobs open to women with only homemaking experience. Live-in housekeepers and live-in companions are particularly needed. Also appropriate for former housewives is work in the housekeeping departments of hospitals, institutions, or hotels. Unfortunately, the non-supervisory jobs in these areas pay very little, if anything, above the minimum wage.

Of course, women with office skills can easily find better paying jobs in business. Even in the current recession and tight labor market, the demand for experienced clerical help is high. A good typist, stenographer, or bookkeeper can be assured of finding rewarding work. If working in an office appeals to you but you do not have these skills, consider taking a short training course to acquire them. Experts have found that office skills can be learned at any age. Instruction at your local business school, community college, or adult education center will put you in a good position to find work. Remember that employers usually require 40 to 60 words a minute for typing speed and 80 to 90 words a minute in dictation. So if you have these skills but they are rusty, it will pay to take a refresher course to bring them up to the required level.

Another area where women appear to have greater acceptance than men is in factory operator jobs. The apparel industry particularly employs a great number of older women. Hotels, retail stores, and beauty salons are also good places for women to look for work. And of course, nursing jobs are still readily available for those women who can qualify.

ANALYZE YOUR BACKGROUND

If you are unsure of the kind of work for which you are best suited, give it some thought. Do not plan to approach prospective employers with, "I'm looking for any kind of work." This will rarely get you anything. If by chance it does get a response, be assured it will be only an offer of a menial job at beginning-level pay, a job which the employer has most likely found impossible to fill or keep filled. If you want more than that, you must have a direction. It will help if you take the time to look at your background and analyze it.

A good way to do this is to write down your complete personal history. This is for your eyes alone. It will not only be the basis on which you will choose your retirement work, it will also help you prepare your job résumé later. It will even help you conduct your job interviews more effectively and generally assist you in selling your services. Make it complete. Start with your school years and write down everything you can remember about your activities, your interests, your hobbies, and your jobs. Do not forget unpaid employment. Good work habits are formed in homemaking or volunteer work and many employers recognize that. List what you did, when you did it, why you did it, and how much responsibility you had. A woman should also list any help she gave her husband with his work. For example, did you help him send out bills, do research, or keep his company books? I know a woman of 63 who was able to get a job as a legal secretary because she capitalized on her knowledge of legal jargon which she had learned helping her lawyer husband with his "homework."

After you have completed your history, look it over and question yourself about which jobs you liked and why. Which duties did you perform best? Do you work best with your hands? Your head? Or are you best in human relations? Such a self-analysis will help you be realistic about your strong and weak points and pinpoint the type of work you should seek. Think of every type of job in which your interest and experience would be useful to employers in your community. Remember that liabilities in one type of work may be assets in another. Ask yourself, "For what kind of jobs does my background best qualify me?" It might be advisable for you to look over the *Dictionary of Occupational Titles* which is available at all state employment offices and public libraries. This book lists over 20,000 job titles and descriptions. Perhaps it will help you locate some new types of jobs for which you are qualified or which appeal to you. Here is a piece of advice from a gentleman of 88 who switched into his present job, full-time acting, at the age of 67. He says, "Don't be afraid to try new things. I learned five jobs after I was 57."

Investigate all jobs which interest you and also look into related fields. A good source for such research is the *Occupational Outlook Handbook*, published by the Bureau of Labor Statistics, U.S. Department of Labor, also available at your public library.

NEED FOR MORE EDUCATION

Appraise your educational background. Was your schooling obtained too many years ago or was it of too brief a duration for the requirements in today's job market? If you wish to change your occupation, do you have all the necessary education? You may need a high school diploma, the educational level now set as the basic requirement for a vast number of job openings.

While older people have knowledge and wisdom gained from years of practical living and experience, many lack sufficient schooling. Their relative lack of formal education in comparison with that of younger persons today aggravates their problem of finding work. A study of the educational backgrounds of different age groups found that half of those 65 or over have not completed elementary school. At the same time, three-fourths of all men between 25 and 29 have a high school education. Of course this is the net result of the steady advances in public education made in this country. Each succeeding generation has been exposed to a more extensive education, so that today's senior citizens in the aggregate have fallen behind in educational level. The changing nature of jobs because of technological advances and the rising level of mass education have raised employers' educational requirements and preferences. Thus, the level of education becomes quite significant when one is looking for post-retirement work. For instance, the number of retirees with extensive education still working into their 70s is high in comparison with other less educated groups.

Besides suffering deficiencies in formal education, many elderly have not kept up with advances in their field. Those continuing on the same job for many years often are able to get by on outdated information. But once out of work and looking for a new position, they are quickly pegged as "old hat" and not hired. Many then find themselves qualified only for some unskilled job. And if a tight labor market comes along, the unskilled and semi-skilled positions become scarce and these persons have more difficulty finding work than most. On the other hand, professionally trained and skilled individuals have the advantage. They have something to offer employers as the competition gets keener. At such times, we know that employers become more selective and demanding. For example, many businesses today ask that typists be able to type 55 words a minute, where 40 words a minute used to be considered adequate. And as the costs of training workers on the job rises, many employers, no longer willing to incur such expense, look for workers who can be productive immediately.

Job counselors observe that even during a business recession when few job vacancies appear, good jobs still go begging for qualified personnel to fill them. Today in the industrial field there still are many requests for skilled machinists, autobody repairmen, auto mechanics, glaziers, furniture refinishers, and screw machine operators. In the professional area, the data processing and accounting fields are active. As for office work, secretaries, stenographers, and bookkeepers are, as always, easily placed. When applying for these jobs, older workers find that if they have a skill an employer needs, their age is inconsequential. If the employer estimates that they will be able to perform more effectively than younger workers who apply, they will be hired. Therefore, many elderly are going back to school to learn new skills or to polish up old ones, as well as to extend their formal education. Fortunately, many new avenues now exist for older persons to do this at minimal cost. In the following section I will describe some educational programs appropriate for older adults but many more are available. The Academy for Educational Development, Inc., 680 Fifth Avenue, New York, N.Y. 10019, and the Adult Education Association, 810 18th Street, N.W., Washington, D.C. 20006, are both compiling comprehensive lists. These organizations, as well as your state Office on the Aging, should be able to direct you to educational courses in your locality.

EDUCATIONAL PROGRAMS AVAILABLE

The federal government has established a number of training programs which are available to unemployed and poor persons of all ages, but give special consideration to persons over 45 years of age. One such program, called JOBS, is operated under the Manpower Development and Training Act by the U.S. Department of Labor. It executes contracts with employers who train workers on the job and then employ them on a permanent basis. Classroom training in job skills is also available under the Act. The Public Service Careers Program (PSC) and the Public Employment Program (PEP) are two others developed by the government. They provide entry level government jobs designed to teach skills and provide upgrading for the low-income workers participating. A wide range of jobs are involved, covering occupations in public works, transportation, education, law enforcement, and health care. Some of the trainees are kept on as permanent employees and efforts are made to find outside employment for the others. To locate these programs in your area, contact your local state employment office.

In some communities, local jurisdictions have also set up training programs especially for older workers. The Arkansas Department of Labor at Hot Springs sponsored one such program. It enrolled only persons over 45; many were over age 60. The courses were organized as workshops in which the students were able to practice the fundamental techniques of their new occupations under the guidance of experts in each field. To determine which courses to offer, a simple analysis was made in the community of job vacancies which lacked well-trained applicants. Most of these were found to be in the sales and service occupations. As a result, courses were offered in industrial selling, retailing, practical nursing, waitress and waiter training, and floral designing, to name just a few. It is reported that 90 percent of the older workers trained in the program to date have subsequently been employed in the business community.

A similar program at Miami-Dade Community College, called Project Elderly's Oasis, was initiated with private foundation funds. Oasis is an acronym for The Older Adult Seeking Interdisciplinary Studies. After surveying the Miami, Florida, area to determine the work available to older persons, the college is endeavoring to build a model curriculum which will train the elderly for the job market. College fees are waived for those who meet the financial qualifications.

A program of particular interest is the series of Informational-Education courses offered by the Senior Citizens Council of Cass County in Indiana. Taking an informal approach, they organized seminars, workshops, and field trips into the community in order to provide the senior citizen participants with an opportunity to search out areas where they could use their talents and experience.

The previous programs are special ones available only in selected areas, but standard in most communities are the adult education courses offered in the public schools. Basic education courses in English, history, civics, economics, general science, business, and mathematics are generally offered at minimal cost. Often a special course to prepare students for the high school equivalency test is also available. Classes giving training in skills, such as laboratory techniques, key punch operation, typing, stenography, and bookkeeping attract many elderly students. Particularly popular with women are home-care and practical nursing courses. Men favor salesmanship, skilled trades, crafts, and retailing courses. In some communities these courses are even offered in retirement communities, churches, and local social clubs where older people can more easily congregate.

Sometimes federal funds supplement the local budget and make possible special teaching arrangements appropriate for older adults. In Lubbock, Texas, such financing created the Adult Learning Center to foster individual education up to the high school level by letting students proceed at their own speed and choose any subjects they like or feel they need. One participant is a retired carpenter's helper of 87 who had quit school in the fifth grade. Reregistered now at the local elementary school, he comments, "I think the program is wonderful and would recommend it to any senior citizen, I used to be a good speller, but it's gotten away from me over the years. I can't even write a decent letter now, but I'm working on it."

Recently several states have passed laws permitting persons over 60 to take tuition-free courses on a non-credit basis at state universities and community colleges if space is available. A high school diploma is not required of these non-matriculated older students and there is no grading or examination of them. Some institutions, such as the University of Denver, Seattle Pacific College, Ohio State University, Portland State University, and the University of Pittsburgh, have opened credit courses to the elderly at a nominal charge.

In New Jersey, Fairleigh Dickinson University has established a program called the Educational Program for Senior Citizens. It offers tuition-free courses in all subjects for persons 65 or older. There are no entrance requirements and the courses can be taken on either a credit or non-credit basis.

In New York, Hunter College has trained retired policemen and firemen for jobs as nurses. Hunter recently received a private grant to establish a new program called the Brookdale Center on Aging to help broaden their academic program for older adults. For persons over 65 enrolled at Hunter, a Senior Students Center will be established to provide special space and counseling facilities to advise on course selection and second career choices.

The City University of New York operates an Institute of Study for Older Adults which enrolled 5,000 senior citizens in the last semester. One freshman was 84 years old. Classes are offered at seventy different locations for the convenience of older people who will not travel long distances. Also in New York City, Fordham University's College at Sixty offers non-credit interdisciplinary seminars for the retired. The intimate settings of these seminars help the elderly ease into the atmosphere of the academic world. After successfully completing this phase, the students are then automatically admitted to the regular degree program.

Several colleges offer courses designed to help older persons who contemplate a change of occupation to make some realistic choices. In one course on mid-career changes, 31 percent of the students were found to be in the wrong fields to begin with and they were interested and qualified for at least two other fields which would give them greater job satisfaction. George Washington University School of Medicine and Health Sciences in Washington, D.C., has a program called "Second Careers—New Opportunities in Allied Health" in which participants examine health care issues and second career opportunities in health, public health, and mental health fields. Included are group and individual sessions during which students are counseled on the psychological aspects of late-life career changes.

One of the most imaginative programs is a federally supported experiment at the Fairhaven College, a division of Western Washington State College, at Bellingham, Washington. Designed to develop an integrated education community, it is called the Bridge Project, shortened from "bridging the generation gap." Older students there, ranging in age from 60 to 80, pay modest fees to live on campus in a dormitory and take courses on a non-competitive basis without grading. To enhance the multigenerational aspect of the program, a day care center for preschoolers is located in the same building. In addition to attending classes, lectures, plays and concerts at the college, the oldsters help out in the day care center. They are also expected to provide guidance and perspective for the younger college students on campus.

Belief in the idea of life-long learning has prompted a number of universities and schools to offer home-study courses. Often these schools are willing to give older students academic credit for work experience, thus speeding the way to a degree or certificate. The University of Oklahoma offers home-study courses on both the college and high school levels (Independent Study Department, Norman, Oklahoma 73069). Students need only appear for examinations, which may be taken at any convenient college or university where proper supervision can be arranged. The University of Syracuse (University College, 610 East Fayette Street, Syracuse, New York 13202) has a home-study program in the liberal arts for a Bachelor of Arts degree, and a business administration course leading to a Bachelor of Science. Interviews and testing are required for admission, after which students and teachers communicate through the mails and by phone. Students come to the campus twice each year for final examinations, and attend a three-week seminar in the summer. Financial assistance may be available to cover tuition costs. Even advanced degrees are now available through home study. The Doctor of Philosophy degree, for example, is offered at the Union Graduate School of the Union for Experimenting Colleges and Universities in Yellow Springs, Ohio.

For an extensive list of accredited home-study schools teaching everything from audio electronics to writing, ask for the free booklet "Careers for the Homebound" from the B'nai B'rith Career and Counseling Services, 1640 Rhode Island Avenue, N.S., Washington, D.C. 20036.

With all these educational opportunities available, I urge you to consider them. Armed with a recent scholastic degree or some current formal instruction, the older worker has improved his chances for finding employment. The initiative and determination of such action in itself tells a prospective employer that you are "with it." I know that the prospect of returning to school frightens many older persons. They wonder whether they are still able to learn. The fact of the matter is that school records bulge with case histories of persons over 60, and even over 90, who have successfully completed courses of instruction. A survey of 2,000 retirees in California found that more than 30 percent were capable of handling a college curriculum. Other recent evidence verifies that the ability to learn changes little with age. One study found that the potential of persons of 50 and 60 to learn was equal to that at age 16!

I found the following remarks of two elderly students quite to the point: One, an elderly lady struggling through a course in beginning-level Spanish, commented, "I took Spanish because languages are very hard for me. The brain is a muscle. If you don't exercise it, it goes slack." The other, a 100-year-old gentleman attending courses at a community college, reacted this way, "I'm learning things I thought I used to know." And finally let me urge you on with a quote from Henry Ford, "Anyone who stops learning is old, whether this happens at twenty or eighty. Anyone who keeps on learning not only remains young but becomes constantly more valuable, regardless of physical capacity."

3

GETTING HELP FROM THE GOVERNMENT

To start your job search, I want you to be informed about what government programs exist to employ you, even though only a small number of you will want or qualify for these jobs. In order to apply for most of them, your income must be below the federally designated poverty level. Furthermore, not all communities are authorized to offer these programs, and in those areas where they exist, only a comparatively small number of jobs are available because of limited funding. However, those who qualify and are subsequently employed find the work quite stimulating and personally rewarding.

Several programs designed specifically to utilize the services of older persons as volunteers or paid workers are sponsored by federal, state, and local governments. The jobs are mostly of an unskilled or semi-skilled nature, and payment, where made, is rarely above the federal minimum wage. For communities to establish the programs funded by the federal government, contracts are made with selected state and local organizations which want to sponsor the activity. It is primarily in cities and depressed rural areas, where jobs for older persons are particularly scarce, that local community groups come forward to apply for the federal funding. As a result, most of the programs which offer paid employment have a waiting list of applicants. Yet a few communities have recently reported that some of the authorized jobs are going unfilled because not enough residents can meet the very low income requirements. To find out if any of the programs exist in your area and whether there are openings, check with your state Office on Aging (addresses appear in the Appendix) or your state employment office. The specific agencies listed under each program heading below can also give you the information.

ACTION PROGRAMS

The federal agency called ACTION administers the Foster Grandparent Program and the Senior Companion Program.

Foster Grandparent Program. This program, initiated by the Administration on Aging, provides for 20 hours of employment a week for low income persons over 60. Thirty-eight percent of all foster grandparents are past their 70th birthday. In 1975 income maximums for participation were set at $3,062 for a single person and $3,982 for a couple. A non-taxable stipend of $1,670 a year is paid for four hours of work a day, five days a week. Nationwide, about 12,000 persons can be employed under the Foster Grandparent program.

The duties are simply to give love and attention to institutionalized or other needy children. Foster grandparents are assigned to schools for retarded or disturbed children, infant homes, temporary care centers, convalescent hospitals, and Head Start centers. They read to the children, play with them, or take them out into the community and for strolls in the park. The elderly are not intended to replace regular staff at the various institutions but rather to add the element of a person-to-person relationship. They give the children the kind of love often missing in a group-care setting. The duties are particularly attractive to former housewives and mothers who have no skills to offer the business community. The program, however, also employs men; one foster grandparent in five is a foster grandfather.

Besides the wages, foster grandparents receive an annual physical examination paid for by the government, and carfare or transportation to the work site. A short orientation and in-service training period is given participants during which regular wages are paid. A hot midday meal and uniforms are also provided in some areas.

The foster grandparents receive and treasure the trust and

affection of the children involved. Here is how two of the participants perceive their work. A widow who works at a children's hospital with a crippled 14-year-old boy who has no family says, "Everybody's really proud of me, it's one of the greatest things. It gives the greatest satisfaction that I'm wanted there and useful there." A California woman of 104 who cares for two mentally retarded foster grandchildren aged 7 and 9 declares, "Kids keep me young."

Senior Companion Program. This program was established in July, 1974, and is just now becoming operational. It also employs only low income men and women over the age of 60. The income maximums are the same as for the Foster Grandparent Program—$3,062 for a single person, $3,982 if married. The work is to help adults with special needs, such as the elderly, in their own homes, in nursing homes, or in other institutions. Two hours a day, five days a week of work are required, and a non-taxable stipend of $1.60 an hour, free lunch, and up to $1.25 a day for transportation are paid. Only 865 positions nationwide in 18 projects were planned for in the 1975 federal budget.

For further information or to find out whether these programs exist in your area, write to ACTION, 806 Connecticut Avenue, N.W., Washington, D.C. 20525.

DEPARTMENT OF LABOR PROGRAMS

The Manpower Administration of the U.S. Department of Labor has developed some special programs for older workers in cooperation with the National Council of Senior Citizens, the National Council on the Aging, the National Farmers Union, and the American Association for Retired Persons, four organizations that represent or work with the elderly. Formerly financed under Operation Mainstream, they are now funded under the Comprehensive Employment and Training Act of 1973 (CETA), with the current level of funding sufficient to provide jobs for 25,000 people. The various programs are known as Green Thumb, Green Light, Senior Aides, and Senior Community Service Project, and are found primarily in rural areas and towns. They employ needy, chronically unemployed men and women, giving them work designed to improve the communities where they live. It is estimated that over 60 percent of the current participants had yearly incomes below $2,000 before they came into these programs. Enrollees are paid at least the federal minimum wage for up to 40 hours of work a week.

The programs have frequently had a great deal of impact on those who have participated in them. For example, in Monterey, Tennessee, 90 older men are at work, some for the first time in years, tapping a mountain spring and laying pipe to the center of a hamlet a half mile away. On completion the residents will no longer have to haul their water from a town three miles away. Another project enabled Menominee Indians in Wisconsin to open small industries that produce park benches, tables, and handicrafts.

Green Thumb. Sponsored by the National Farmers Union, Project Green Thumb employs low income persons, usually men, over the age of 55. The work performed by the Green Thumbers—some in their 90s—trains them for jobs as gardeners, landscapers, nurserymen, and highway maintenance workers. As a result, some go on to jobs with private firms. In the program, they work to beautify highways, build parks and recreation areas, improve drainage, decrease air and water pollution, restore historical sites, rehabilitate housing, and put their skills to work on other conservation and community betterment projects. In New York a comparable state program was designed to employ 150 Green Thumbers during 1975 by the state Department of Environmental Conservation to monitor air quality, tend the stock at fish hatcheries, compile data for environmental directories, and guide children through environmental education centers.

The national program totals about 3,000 jobs in all and is available in 25 states and Puerto Rico. Payment is at least the federal minimum wage for three days of work a week. A required physical examination is paid for by the program. To be eligible, a worker's income must meet poverty guidelines; screening is done by the local state employment offices.

A Green Thumb participant from Arkansas voiced his feelings about the program. "I think it is the best program for the rural senior citizen. Green Thumb is just like a man getting married and having children to carry on his name. By the same token, we Green Thumbers create something for the coming generation to enjoy and remember us by. This program has changed our outlook on life. Once more we feel that somebody cares." One Green Thumber of Lakewood, New Jersey, credits the program for "a whole new life." A former chicken farmer, he recalls, "When the farm failed, my life was over. At 68, what could I do? I was finished. This program takes people who thought life was over and makes them into men again. Their health improves. It gives them a reason to get up in the morning. It prolongs their lives." A 78-year-old former Trenton, New Jersey, steelworker, out of work for 19 years because of a heart condition, today heads a nine-man crew of Green Thumbers who help beautify Trenton's parks. He says, "I've got a home. If it wasn't for Green Thumb, I would have lost it. It's a lifesaver to us old men who want to work." In Branchburg, New Jersey, the range of work is being broadened by Somerset County College where Green Thumbers are employed in a babysitting service for student mothers. It is an ideal solution to the problem posed by the increasing number of young mothers attending classes. Volunteer student aides are assigned to assist the elderly sitters. "This is a vacation for me to get over there and see the children and the countryside," says Mrs. L., a widow who rarely got out of her house in the last four years. The extra income, which Mrs. L. tucks away "for a rainy day," gives her a sense of independence, she says, adding, "I love the children. This fills my life."

Green Light. Another program sponsored by the National Farmers Union is Green Light. It employs low income rural people 55 or older. Paid at least the federal minimum wage, Green Light employees serve as aides in community services, and through special outreach projects, help to make these services available to the handicapped, the sick, the elderly, and the shut-in. Because of the nature of Green Light jobs, the program attracts more women than men. These projects operate in the rural areas of about eleven states.

Senior Aides. The National Council of Senior Citizens sponsors the Senior Aides program in 53 communities across the country. In this program, 2,800 older workers help with public service activities. As with the other programs, Senior Aides must meet the poverty income guidelines. They work 20 hours a week (4 hours a day, 5 days a week) and earn at least the federal minimum wage. In some areas they also receive transportation to their place of work. The jobs are in hospitals, schools, and day care centers, and the duties might be to provide health assistance, teach arts and crafts, or visit and give meals to the aged and infirm. Some of the communities which have this program are: Allegheny County, Pennsylvania; Boston, Massachusetts; Bridgeport, Connecticut; Buffalo-Jamestown, New York; Chicago, Illinois; Dade County, Florida; Dayton, Ohio; Denver, Colorado; Marion County, West Virginia; Memphis, Tennessee; Milwaukee, Wisconsin; Minneapolis, Minnesota; Newark, New Jersey; New Bedford–Fall River, Massachusetts; Oakland, California; Providence, Rhode Island; St. Louis, Missouri; San Diego, California; and Washington, D.C.

Senior Community Service Project. Under the auspices of the National Council on the Aging and the American Association of Retired Persons/National Retired Teachers Association, the Senior Community Service Project employs low income men and women 55 and older in health and social service jobs. Working part-time, they are paid the federal minimum wage or more depending on the duties. Some assist in rehabilitation and work therapy, help shut-ins, provide cultural programs and other services at senior citizen centers, or search out the elderly poor and tell them about the services and facilities available to them. Still others work as recreation and teacher aides, helping in libraries and counseling children.

Because of the nature of the work assignments, this program is very attractive to those people who have not worked for a long time and therefore do not feel equipped to go out into the job market. Yet after a short period as an aide, many regain their confidence and find full-time jobs in the business community. The program has been particularly effective in showing the employability of those older persons previously regarded as unemployable. Here are examples of the work being done under the Senior Community Service Project: In Maine, aides are assigned to community action agencies to help certify people for surplus food. At the Neighborhood Legal Assistance Society in Los Angeles, California, aides help persons, particularly the elderly, who apply to the agency for assistance in resolving problems with other agencies, groups, and landlords. Aides in San Antonio, Texas, counsel youthful offenders at the juvenile detention center on a one-to-one basis. An aide who was formerly a beautician has "reached" girls who are normally very difficult to handle by providing grooming classes and beauty treatments. Enrollees in Paintsville, Kentucky, are part of a team repairing homes of the elderly poor. Under the auspices of the University of Vermont, aides in St. Albans are interviewing and canvassing rural elderly consumers to determine their specific needs. Aides in Hoboken, New Jersey, are assigned as bilingual aides in city elementary school classrooms to help Spanish-speaking children to read, write, and speak English.

Some of the other areas where Senior Community Service Projects are conducted are: Phoenix, Arizona; Colton, San Francisco, and Stockton in California; Trenton, New Jersey; Albany, Binghamton, Bronx, Canton, Hempstead, and White Plains in New York; Portland, Oregon; Carlisle, Philadelphia, Scranton, and York in Pennsylvania; Brownsville, Texas; and Huntington, West Virginia.

For more specific information and addresses of these programs, write to the Regional Manpower Administrator of the U.S. Department of Labor at the appropriate address listed on page 45.

In addition to these programs, the Department of Labor has granted funds to Alaska, Delaware, and Hawaii for their own employment programs under the Older American Community Service Employment Act. For information on these

REGIONAL OFFICES OF THE MANPOWER ADMINISTRATION

Location	States Served	
Room 1703 John F. Kennedy Fed. Bldg. Boston, MA 02203	Connecticut Maine Massachusetts	New Hampshire Rhode Island Vermont
Room 3713 1515 Broadway New York, N.Y. 10036	New Jersey New York	
P.O. Box 8796 Philadelphia, PA 19101	Delaware Maryland Pennsylvania	Virginia West Virginia
D.C. Manpower Administrator Room 220, District Building 14th and E Streets, NW Washington, D.C. 20004	District of Columbia	
Room 405 1371 Peachtree Street, NE Atlanta, GA 30309	Alabama Florida Georgia Kentucky	Mississippi North Carolina South Carolina Tennessee
300 South Wacker Drive Chicago, IL 60606	Illinois Indiana Michigan	Minnesota Ohio Wisconsin
1100 Commerce Street Dallas, TX 75202	Arkansas Louisiana New Mexico	Oklahoma Texas
Room 3000, Federal Building 911 Walnut Street Kansas City, MO 64106	Iowa Kansas	Missouri Nebraska
Room 16015, Federal Office Building 1961 Stout Street Denver, CO 80202	Colorado Montana North Dakota	South Dakota Utah Wyoming
450 Golden Gate Avenue Box 36084 San Francisco, CA 94102	Arizona California	Hawaii Nevada
Room 2154, Arcade Plaza 1321 Second Avenue Seattle, WA 98101	Alaska Idaho	Oregon Washington

programs, check with the appropriate U.S. Department of Labor regional office.

EMERGENCY EMPLOYMENT

The Emergency Jobs and Unemployment Assistance Act of 1974 endeavors to help workers cope with the business recession. This act specifically includes persons over 45 who desire to remain in, enter, or reenter the labor work force. At least $2.5 billion has been allocated to provide public service jobs, mostly in areas of high unemployment. The program, run by the local jurisdictions which define the jobs and decide who will fill them, usually includes such jobs as ambulance attendant, dog catcher, youth counselor, process server, clerk-typist, and school crossing guard.

For information on these jobs in your locality, contact your state employment office or write to your Regional Manpower Administrator of the U.S. Department of Labor.

LEGISLATIVE INTERN

Jobs as Congressional interns which were previously filled only by students are now being filled by people of 65 and over. Representative Edward G. Biester, Jr., Republican of Pennsylvania, was the first to try the idea in 1972. Now a dozen or more representatives and senators have appointed over-65 interns to their staffs.

Some state legislators are also availing themselves of the services of interns in the over-65 age category. Owing to the transportation problems, participation in these jobs is usually confined to the elderly who already live in the state capital. Some of the duties assigned to the elderly interns have been to assist with mail from elderly constituents, participate in meetings on topics of interest to older people, report back to their home communities on legislation pending, and explain enacted laws which affect them. Hours and wages for these jobs vary. Ask your state and federal representatives for information.

RETIRED MILITARY

The U.S. Department of Defense had a program to aid retired servicemen in entering second careers. It consisted of a counseling service and a computerized man-job matching system. The program assisted the retiree in coping with the realities of an employment search and helped to reduce his floundering, indecision, and uncertainty. Unfortunately, the program was abolished by Congress at the end of 1972. Letters requesting the reinstatement of the program should be addressed to your Congressional representatives or to the Office of the Assistant Secretary of Defense, Washington, D.C. 20301.

LOCAL PROGRAMS

A variety of programs have been established for senior citizens by local communities. Here are some examples of community programs:

In the public schools in Dade County, Florida, elderly teacher aides are paid to perform a wide variety of non-instructional tasks, in support of both teachers and pupils, helping to improve the educational programs.

Senior citizen library aides in Vermont make it possible for the public libraries, particularly in rural areas, to remain open longer.

Senior citizens in Michigan work as tourist guides in the summer to show visitors the scenic views, and to point out the good fishing and excellent camping sites.

The Department of Recreation in New York City has hired senior citizens as paraprofessionals to take over some of the duties of the department's professional staff. They work in recreation programs designed for other senior citizens and are paid the minimum wage for 14 hours a week.

In Smithtown, New York, a town program called Senior Citizens Job Placement Program is a cooperative effort of the State Commerce Department, the Smithtown Recreation Department, and a local aerospace parts manufacturer. It provides hundreds of jobs for the elderly, paying $2.50 to

$4.40 an hour depending on prior experience. Residents 60 years of age or older are screened by the town for the positions, which involve working on the assembly line.

The city of Miami, Florida, has hired older people to work in clerical positions in the police department. In the initial phase, 32 workers aged 54 to 68 were hired as part-time clerks and typists. As a result, trained policemen are released from clerical duties to provide improved protection on the streets.

If you are interested in any of the above programs, contact your state Office on the Aging or the specific local departments referred to above.

CIVIL SERVICE EMPLOYMENT

Those interested in regular government employment under the civil service system should be aware that many state and local governments set 70 as their mandatory retirement age. If you are below 70, check with the appropriate personnel department for information on the testing dates for positions, or the availability of non-competitive vacancies for which no examinations are required. You are no doubt aware that patronage is still firmly entrenched in local governments, so non-competitive jobs are quite often filled through political clubs. Therefore the best way to local government employment may be through the political organization of your choice. Even if you have not had any previous contact with the political system, it may pay you to do so now. As a suggestion, write to the local representative of your state legislature, or county governing body. You will most certainly receive a courteous reply and you may be surprised by even more concrete help. Referral to the local personnel officer may be forthcoming. Such an introduction will carry some weight and might very well result in a job offer from him. At the same time, you may want to take whatever examinations are being given. Of course, processing of lists takes time so do not expect an offer of a position before almost a year has passed.

In the federal government, there is no official maximum

age limit, but only persons under 70 can qualify for regular appointments. Those over 70 can receive only temporary positions, subject to annual renewal. The U.S. Government is one of the largest employers of older persons. Of the 2,900,000 federal employees, some 230,000 or 8 percent are 60 or older. There are government jobs of almost every type and occupation—engineers, maintenance men, typists, messengers, doctors, lawyers, etc. There are temporary, part-time, and seasonal, as well as full-time, jobs. While most appointments are made from test lists, in some occupations appointments are made only on the basis of an evaluation of qualifications. It is not necessary to live in Washington, D.C., for jobs become available in every state. However, at present because of current budget limitations, federal job opportunities are few for workers of all ages. Still, because of the excellent fringe benefits in government—vacations, holidays, insurance—it may be worth your while to apply at the nearest office of the U.S. Civil Service Commission.

4

GETTING HELP FROM EMPLOYMENT SERVICES

Almost everyone looking for a job applies to an employment agency some time during the search, with good reason, since these services provide an effective marketplace for employers and prospective employees to find each other. In addition, they usually act to screen out undesirable employers and provide a clear description of job openings and qualification requirements, saving the applicant time which otherwise would be wasted on interviews for inappropriate jobs. For the elderly applicant, however, these services are not a cut-and-dried matter. This chapter will try to make you more knowledgeable of the services available to you and to steer you to those agencies which can be of most help, those which know the problems you face and understand how to deal with them.

U.S. AND STATE EMPLOYMENT SERVICE

Jobseekers are most familiar with the U.S. Employment Service, which operates some 2,400 offices in affiliation with state employment services. Just about every industrial area in the country is covered by these publicly-funded employment agencies. Besides job placement they offer counseling, testing, and training referral, all free of charge. Many of the offices maintain "job banks," which are computerized lists of job vacancies in the community. These "job banks" contain pertinent information concerning all job vacancies registered with the service in the particular area. After the data is compiled, updated, and fed into a computer, the print-outs are distributed periodically to the various offices concerned.

In the operation of the "job bank" system, an individual

seeking work may study the list of job vacancies and compare his own qualifications with requirements of various specific positions listed. The system is of considerable help to an applicant, permitting him to choose for himself those job openings which interest him. However, for those elderly who need counseling or advice in their job search, the state employment offices are not apt to be very helpful. For though the service offers a good deal of assistance to the average unemployed worker, the older applicant is frequently ignored. This happens because most offices of state employment services lack sufficient personnel to give the elderly the extra attention needed to place them. And very often the counselors do not possess the specialized knowledge needed to effectively work with the older job seeker. However, a few offices of the state employment services now employ staff members, called "older worker specialists," who are trained in the placement and counseling of workers over 45. These specialists offer testing, training referral, and related services. In order to stimulate more job openings, they canvass employers and advise them concerning the skills, productivity, and potential of older workers.

Since people over 65 are not covered by the federal Age Discrimination in Employment Act, the elderly do not legally have to be a priority for job placement. Thus, while persons of all ages may avail themselves of the U.S. employment service, those over 65 are not in the primary area of concern. Even the older worker specialists are likely to reflect this and devote more time to persons under 65 who are still in the labor market.

COMMERCIAL EMPLOYMENT AGENCIES

Similarly, the elderly applicant will usually find that placing an application with a private employment agency will not bring results either. Because private services are profit-oriented, they shun the time-consuming and therefore expensive task of finding employment for older workers. In fact, many commercial agencies refuse to accept applications from anyone over 60.

EMPLOYMENT SERVICES FOR THE ELDERLY

However, there are special agencies which fill this void and which work only with the elderly, the best known being Mature Temps, Inc. Endorsed by the American Association of Retired Persons and the National Retired Teachers Association, Mature Temps has branches in Atlanta; Baltimore; Boston; Chicago; East Orange, New Jersey; Houston; Los Angeles; Minneapolis; New York City; Philadelphia, Pittsburgh, and Plymouth, Pennsylvania; San Francisco; St. Louis; and Washington, D.C., and other cities.

Mature Temps is a profit-making organization and operates like the typical commercial temporary help agency, with the important difference that it specializes in handling older workers. Like the temporary help agencies, this service places the applicant on its own payroll and bills the employer for the work performed plus a service charge. Mature Temps then pays the employee his salary, taking care of Social Security costs, insurance, and other fringe benefits. This organization has been quite successful in placing older applicants. Not all who apply to Mature Temps, however, are accepted. Rigorous examinations are given in the skills most in demand by employers in the area. Usually typing, steno, and knowledge of other clerical and office operations are required. Only applicants who pass tests in these skills are placed on the agency's list. In some offices of Mature Temps, persons with professional training, such as engineers, accountants, and sales executives, are accepted for placement in addition to clerical personnel.

NON-PROFIT SENIOR CITIZEN EMPLOYMENT SERVICES

The remainder of the chapter will be devoted to the employment services that are of most value to the retiree, the non-profit senior citizen employment services. These organizations, located in numerous communities nationwide, do not pick and choose their applicants but service all elderly who apply. While some set the minimum age at 55, most take anyone who considers himself a senior citizen. Even when age is specified in the name of the agency, such as in 60-Plus or Over-60, younger applicants are still welcome.

Most of these organizations have been established by community organizations, clubs, religious groups, and in several instances, by just a handful of concerned citizens. While some are supported by government funds, most operate with private donations from individuals and businesses, or dues of the sponsoring organizations, making no charge to applicants. For example, the Senior Personnel Placement Bureau, Inc., of Norwalk, Connecticut, was started by a group of retirees. Among the originators of the Bureau was a retired manufacturer, Lawrence Hochheimer, who is still its very active president. Incorporated as a non-profit organization, they were chartered to obtain public and private contributions to carry out their stated purpose of seeking jobs for older persons. With an initial contribution from the Norwalk Chamber of Commerce which provided office space, supplies, a telephone, and some staff assistance, they opened their doors in January, 1966. Their 71-year-old president donated his own money for operating expenses. As they began to show results, they received a grant from the Connecticut Commission on Services for Elderly Persons under the U.S. Older Americans Act. Federal support ended after three years, but financial aid was obtained from local businessmen and others to continue the project. Membership dues and contributions from the Norwalk United Fund now support its work. Elderly volunteer interviewers and clerks help keep expenses low.

Most of the other senior citizen employment agencies currently in operation are also staffed by volunteer retirees, many of whom devote themselves so wholeheartedly to their jobs that applicants who approach them are assured of a sympathetic reception and understanding counsel. This atmosphere is particularly helpful to those elderly who, after being out of work for a period of time, may fear new job situations. The warm, friendly attitude of the volunteers, and their willingness to be of service, goes a long way toward putting timid applicants at ease. Many soon feel ready to face the work situation with a more positive and happy attitude.

To further bolster their confidence, some services send a counselor along with the applicant on his first placement to help smooth over initial problems. They help with the filling out of preliminary papers and the clarification of work instructions, as needed.

How They Operate. While most senior citizen employment services, like the typical commercial employment agency, bring applicant and employer together and then withdraw, a few use the temporary help system typified by Mature Temps, Inc. In this method, the agency charges the employer for the workers they supplied, and the workers are paid by the employment agency from that fee. This procedure has certain advantages when dealing with employers who have mandatory retirement policies. Placing the employee on the payroll of the employment agency permits a business to hire an older worker whose skills it needs without infringing on company rules. In addition, insurance costs, personnel processing, and fringe benefit costs are handled by the agency. Some businesses, in fact, have certain employees, whose services they need, transferred to the employment agency's payroll as they near retirement age, so that they can continue to work without interruption at "retirement." The Senior Personnel Placement Bureau, Inc., of Norwalk, Connecticut, and the New Life Institute of Albertson, New York, employ this method.

The operation of the Senior Workers Service of Spokane, Washington, is unique in that it is located in an office of the state employment service. Though it uses state office space, supplies, and training facilities, it nevertheless functions independently. It was organized by the Greater Spokane Council on Aging to be run by and exclusively for older persons. To attract applicants, this service uses the slogan, "A cordial invitation to those of you who are retiring, but not about to quit." Many of the job applicants offer to volunteer at the desk and subsequently find employment that way. One such case involved a retired school teacher who applied for work, and stayed to help at the senior workers' desk. Oddly enough, the first call she answered was from a private school that had an opening for an instructor to teach commercial subjects, her specialty, one class a day. It was fortunate that she was manning the phone for she had not written all her qualifications on her application. She had mistakenly believed that in her senior years she would no longer find an opening in her own field, but she is now teaching at the school.

The level of operation of most of the senior citizen employment services as they exist today is limited. Some have only one or two permanent employees, although a few are of substantial size. One of the oldest and largest is the Federal Employment and Guidance Service of New York City, established in 1934. Also, the South County Center in Edmonds, Washington, is quite large, using some sixty volunteers in the program. This latter agency, begun in 1968 with four applicants and two job situations and, in the words of its director, "no one terribly interested in hiring senior citizens," today places over 250 persons each month in meaningful jobs. The employment program of the South County Center is one facet of a multi-purpose center where services such as educational classes, recreational activities, transportation, and information and referral programs are also available.

Small employment services, which tend to be located in essentially rural areas, may place only about 20 seniors a month, since commercial establishments are few and therefore job opportunities are limited. Because most retirees prefer to work close to home at jobs that are easily accessible, these agencies must confine their activities to a small area. Most senior citizen employment services, in fact, cover only a single community. In this way, the agency personnel come to know all the employers in the area very well, and the counselors, learning which skills are in demand in the local business area, can guide applicants into fields where their talents have the best chance of being employed.

The boards of directors or advisory committees of these senior citizen employment agencies are also of use in helping to place applicants. Many of these boards are composed of local businessmen and community leaders who can approach members of the business community with ease and on a personal basis, probably the major reason these employment services have been so successful in placing elderly applicants.

Kinds of Jobs Handled. Here is a selection of the jobs which recently were listed at the Senior Skills Foundation, Inc., a senior citizen employment service in West Nyack, New York.

—Apartment house superintendent paying $3.00 an hour but salary is negotiable. Also, handyman needed to paint and clean up apartments for incoming tenants, Mondays through Thursdays.

—Trade association has opening for a public relations manager-director; salary and hours to be negotiated.

—Liquor store seeks a full or part-time clerk at $2.50 an hour for sales and to stock shelves.

—Toolmaker (part-time). Salary and hours open to negotiation. Applicant must have experience in the technology and be able to make models and do tool and die work without supervision. Company is on the bus route.

—Man experienced in electronics wanted by family to teach 2 small boys who are eager to learn the field. Hours are flexible and pay is negotiable.

—School seeks playground aide Mondays through Fridays from 11:15 A.M. to 1:30 P.M. at $2.50 an hour. Duties consist of helping teachers during playground period and doing light office work.

—Home for senior citizens needs someone to operate an audio-visual projector to show sound films every Tuesday from 7 to 9 P.M. Offers minimum wage and will train inexperienced operator.

—Someone needed to cut hedges and mow the lawn for four hours every other week. Employer has own tools and equipment and will pay $2.50 an hour.

—Gal Friday needed for physician's office to answer phone, make appointments, greet patients, and do stenography and typing. Knowledge of making ledger entries desirable. Will pay $3.50 to $3.75 an hour, four days a week.

—Sitter needed to supervise two children, aged 6 and 10,

after they come home from school. Five days a week from 3:30 to 5:30 P.M., for $2 an hour.

—Carpenters (3) needed by contractor to work full or part-time on home improvements. Applicants can choose to put in five days a week or less, as they prefer. $3 an hour.

—Manufacturer of miniature clothing for dogs will pay minimum wage for beginners and more (negotiable) for experienced tailors to lay out and cut patterns and use power sewing machines. Days and hours are flexible, full-time preferred.

—Businessman will train anyone with clerical experience to handle payroll for 16 persons and enter accounts payable, and will pay $3 an hour while learning. Job involves about four hours work once a week.

—Man to fill and ship orders and occasionally make deliveries for optical goods firm. Must have car; business experience helpful. Minimum wage.

—Art gallery looking for man to administer and maintain premises. Hours and pay flexible.

—Investigator-adjuster for insurance claim service. Duties to check on claims, take pictures, etc. Must have car. Payment on per job basis.

—Center for the physically handicapped needs man to visit local businessmen, acquaint them with the work of the center, and locate jobs for the handicapped. Pay negotiable.

—Office assistants, male or female, for retail dress store to keep office work up to date, do labeling and tagging, and check inventory. $3 per hour for 15 hours per week.

—Outside watchmen (2) for plant. Hours from 8 A.M. to 2 P.M. and from 1 to 6 P.M. Salary is negotiable.

In addition to filling existing job vacancies, many of the agencies develop jobs. They probably perform their greatest service in this manner. As one agency director puts it, "For the good jobs, you have to dig." Often lists of available job seekers' skills and abilities are circulated through various channels to solicit jobs. Some agencies even use groups of retired or semi-retired businessmen to make personal contact with local companies, encouraging them to place job openings with the agency. Or agency personnel may visit plants, stores, and offices to find possible openings for clients.

Working on a one-to-one basis, in the manner of an executive search agency, an interviewer can determine an applicant's strong points and then work to develop a job opening, often tailored to his specific talents. Such individualized job development, placement, and intensive counseling can double or triple the chances for the older worker to find a good job. At one service, an applicant who had held a job as a financial manager of a credit union was recently looking for part-time work. The interviewer had no job listings in his profession, but on questioning the applicant found that he had a life-long hobby of stamp collecting. The counselor called a member of the local chamber of commerce associated with the agency, who in turn contacted a stamp dealer who was a personal friend. The dealer needed additional help just then and hired the applicant on the spot. The former financial manager is now enjoying his new career as philatelist more, he says, than he ever enjoyed his former occupation.

In another instance, a former ironworker, who had done electrical welding, layout work, and blueprint reading for twenty-three years in the construction industry, registered with the local senior employment service, never expecting at 69 to find work in his specialty. The counselor called every iron works company listed in the local telephone directory and located one that was interested in the applicant. At the interview the ironworker was surprised and pleased to learn that his prospective employer was a former business acquaintance who was striking out on his own. The employer in turn was delighted to hire the ironworker with whose skills he was familiar.

Here are some other examples of individuals placed by senior citizen employment services:

—A Japanese gentleman in his early 70s needed additional income. When the agency's interviewer found that he knew three dialects of Japanese as well as several other languages, a part-time position was quickly found for him at a nearby university which maintains a language bank.

—A secretary of 62 had worked 15 years for one company. She was very despondent, believing that no one would hire her because of her age. But she was referred to a position as a church secretary and got the job.

—A former automobile salesman of 63 was placed as a club manager for a local women's organization.

—Another man who had worked for 17 years as an instrument inspector and supervisor in a receiving department obtained a part-time job as salesman in a local department store. He had owned a men's clothing business in his native Germany many years before, and was able, in retirement, to again put to use his knowledge of men's clothing.

—A 65-year-old man had worked as an investigator of fraudulent visas for the State Department. This nearly stumped the employment service counselor, but the man was finally placed in a job as the manager of a small tennis club.

—The interviewer was startled by an 86-year-old man who beat his fist on the desk, saying, "This is the first time I've been out of work in 67 years. I want a job." He was placed as a night guard in a manufacturing plant.

Other Services Performed. Some agencies have opened up whole new fields of employment for the elderly. Concentrating particularly on those applicants who do not have salable skills, the services offer them training in the kind of jobs that are needed in the community. An example is the Good Neighbor or Family Aide Training Program operated by the Over–60 Counseling and Employment Service in Montgomery County, Maryland, and other agencies. In this program older women are trained to take care of children and older people, and then are placed in jobs close to home. The Maryland agency usually has twelve requests for every available applicant. Explaining the development of the program, the Executive Director of this agency said, "We had lots of job offers in this area and no one to fill them. Nobody wanted to be classified as a domestic." To make sure prospective aides would not be exploited or suffer a loss of pride, the agency has laid out a rigid set of guidelines for training, minimum pay, and kinds of work aides would be expected, and not expected, to do.

The course, which is free of charge, includes practical psychology, environmental health, nutrition, food management, and discussion of the responsibilities of both the aide and the employer. According to the guidelines, "On the job, the Good Neighbor attends to the personal needs of an elderly person or a child, as a companion to the elderly, or as a mother-substitute for the child. She may assist with feeding, bathing, dressing, planning and preparing meals, shopping, and tidying the house but she is not committed to heavy housework or heavy laundry." Professional instructors from the state Department of Mental Hygiene, the Red Cross Nursing Service, and the University Extension Service teach the course. Some of the elderly students are college graduates while some cannot read or write. These are examples of the jobs they receive: A few aides who were placed as housemothers at a university were given free apartments and full maintenance plus $2,600 for a work-year that lasts only 10 months. One "Good Neighbor," Mrs. Rita D., 68, is a companion and aide three days a week to a lively and sharp-witted lady of 80. Mrs. D., a widow for 14 years who never before developed any job skills, now has a job that gives her the money she needs to supplement her small income from Social Security and a veteran's pension.

Another program operated by this Maryland agency is called the Senior Home Craftsman. In this program, training is given in such things as replacing faucet washers, fixing locks, painting, wallpaper hanging, and other handyman jobs too small for commercial firms to handle. This kind of work is particularly suitable for elderly men who have had a lifetime of keeping their own homes in repair. These trainees are also quickly put to work in private homes in their local areas.

Mr. William D., who retired after 35 years with an oil company, has benefited from the Senior Home Craftsman training. He says, "I just wanted something a couple of hours, and they asked me if I was handy and why don't I become a handyman because they have a lot of calls for that type of work. So I said, that sounds good because I've always loved that kind of work." The next thing he knew he was signed up for the craftsman training course. On completion he started repairing neighbors' homes—torn porch screens, kitchen doors that stick, broken window sashes. He earns $3.50 an hour and plans to raise his prices to $5.00 an hour soon.

Here are some other services offered by different senior citizen employment services:

Experience, Inc., of California offers a research, consulting, planning, and advisory service to the community, utilizing the talents of their senior participants in teams. Some of the projects sponsored by the service have been: 1) research and development studies and surveys, data collection and analysis, and product testing; 2) training of state employees, and establishment of a school for drug and alcohol reeducation; 3) production and distribution activities to handle short-term and emergency situations in the community; 4) personal guidance activities for seniors, people about to become seniors, and youths; 5) governmental liaison work to help coordinate functions of local, regional, state, and federal units, especially for programs of public improvement and for older Americans. The members who participate in these projects do so as independent contractors for fees commensurate with services performed and industry rates.

Since many elderly job seekers want part-time employment because of Social Security restrictions, some agencies match and pair two or more workers for a single full-time job by dovetailing the working hours.

Sheltered workshops are operated by a few services. The agency maintains a workplace where the elderly can work on items or services contracted from local employers who have limited space or insufficient workforces for such jobs as labeling, assembling, packaging, hand and machine sewing, and clerical tasks.

It is encouraging to see that just about all senior citizen employment services are experiencing increased support and acceptance from the business community. One service reports a 79 percent increase in placements over a three-year period, with a corresponding tripling of job orders. An employment service in Chattanooga, Tennessee, had more applicants than jobs when it began in 1970, but now its administrator boasts that it can "practically place anyone who wants to work."

Appendix B gives the names and addresses of non-profit employment services in the various states. Besides private organizations, the list includes programs of local Offices for the Aging, which are run on essentially the same basis. From time to time new organizations are formed, so if your community is not listed, check with your state Office on the Aging. (Addresses are given in Appendix A.)

5

FINDING WORK ON YOUR OWN

Locating a job when you are elderly is no easy task. But studies have shown that those older workers who use a wide-ranging approach—application at employment services, answering want ads, direct employer contacts, inquiries of friends and relatives—are the most likely to be successful. Unfortunately, many retirees just register with one of the senior citizen employment agencies and then sit back and wait to be called. While these services have good records of placing their applicants, not one can do a 100 percent job. Therefore it is most desirable that you do some job searching on your own as well.

If you have not job hunted in many moons, you may feel at a loss as to how to begin. You may be unaware that over the past decades procedures and techniques have been developed to make the search shorter and pleasanter. Job hunting has become professionalized and is an art in itself. Yet in this chapter you will find the basic methods simply presented. It will give you the knowledge that will enable you to develop your own job leads. By following through on them, you can locate a job that will meet your specific needs and qualifications.

WHERE TO LOOK

Many of the best jobs are filled soon after the openings develop without ever being advertised or recruited for. People who know about openings tell friends and relations and the good positions are quickly taken off the market. An unusual and effective way of tuning in on this private grapevine was developed in Southern Illinois recently. An ad was placed in a local paper offering a monetary reward to anyone with knowledge of good jobs in a variety of fields. The reward would be paid only if someone was hired. Information poured in. You need not resort to this drastic method, but you should be aware that one of the best and easiest ways of finding work is still by personal recommendation.

Tell your friends, relatives, former business acquaintances, fellow church and club members, and other associates that you are looking for work. Do not be embarrassed to ask for help. Ask any neighbor or acquaintance you believe might have some good business contacts. When approaching them for help, do so in a straightforward manner. Mention several jobs you are best qualified for. Have some definite suggestions as to what you would like the person to do and then present them as tactfully as possible. If you want a friend to write a letter on your behalf, draft a suggested letter, giving him the liberty to change it or write a completely new one if he wishes. If you want your friend to call a prospective employer, hand him the telephone number. Make it easy for him to do it "now."

If your personal contacts do not produce any good prospects, you will have to apply directly to employers, something retirees often hesitate to do. They are afraid of rejection by prospective employers solely on the basis of their age. Many an elderly person has told me, "I don't know which company I can walk into to ask for a job. My age is against me." Do not give in to such thoughts. Have confidence. There are any number of businesses that need your skill; it is merely a question of locating them. Keep in mind that young workers can never compete with you on one thing—your experience. A renowned physician in the field of rehabilitative medicine, in advocating the return to work of older people, remarked, "You can be born brilliant but you cannot be born wise; that only comes with experience and experience comes with time."

Let me help you find the businesses which will not refuse you out of hand, and where you will have a good chance for a job. You should avoid large employers. A great many big companies have rigid retirement policies and therefore flatly refuse to hire persons over 65. A retiree will have better luck by contacting small and medium-sized concerns. The small businessman, the little shopkeeper, the non-profit community organization, and the individual employer are the most receptive to hiring the older worker. Small hotels or motels, retail stores, schools, and personal and medical service firms are good places to look. Many retirees also find work at hospitals, churches, or charitable institutions in their area. Following is a list of possible sources of employment which I suggest you explore:

Banks
Building management firms
Child-care facilities
Churches
Community agencies and services
Factories
Filling stations
Homes for the aged
Hospitals and related institutions
Hotels, motels, resorts
Industrial and commercial associations
Laboratories
Libraries, museums, art galleries
Mail service firms
Market research and survey organizations
Neighborhood services, such as laundries, tailor shops, dry cleaning stores
Parks, beaches, historic sites
Photographic studios
Placement agencies
Private households
Public and private schools
Recreation centers, bowling alleys
Refreshment stands, amusement parks, concessioners
Restaurants, cafeterias, luncheonettes
Sales promotion and canvassing firms
Senior centers
Stores, shopping centers, supermarkets
Tailor shops
Theaters, movie houses

Now let us investigate how best to locate the specific employers in each of these categories. Your first consideration will be commuting, based on what means of transportation are available to you and how far you wish to travel to your work. Older people with diminishing energies often look for short traveling time in order to reserve their strength for on-the-job activities. Daily commuting often becomes quite onerous when done for a long time. So if you are like most retirees, you will be looking for work close to home.

Having decided on the maximum distance you can travel, consider what industries and business firms are located within that area. To augment your personal knowledge, check the classified pages of the telephone directory. Note what retail stores, industries, wholesalers, transportation companies, community agencies, hospitals, and so on, are listed. Check for any firms which could employ your special talents. As you look at the business categories, think of all the different skills they might employ. For example, artists are used by printing firms; security guards work for banks, factories, and stores. Maintenance men, drivers, and accountants are used by any number of businesses. Compile as large a list as you can of firms that could use your skills.

Next, be sure to read the ads and neighborhood business reports of your local nwespaper. You will be alerted to any new companies moving into your area, or any existing ones experiencing increased activity or expansion. Add them to your list to be contacted later. These companies may become your best prospects.

USING WANT ADS EFFECTIVELY

The want ads of your local newspaper are an extremely important part of your job hunt, not only for the obvious reason of locating job vacancies in your field, but to help develop other job leads. Most people do not know how to read want ads effectively. The usual procedure of looking down the list alphabetically for a specific job title has limited value. Have you noticed that there is no consistent terminology? For example, ads starting with any of these words are openings for an office worker: Gal/Man Friday, Experienced, Mature, General office worker, Office supervisor, Part-time clerk, Accounts payable clerk, Administrative assistant, Airline personnel clerk, Figure clerk, File clerk, Insurance clerk, Temporary worker. Or jobs for recreational aides can be listed as "Activity leader assistant." If restaurant work is what you are after, you might find it listed under "Waitress," "Counter help," "Bar maid," "Cocktail waitress," or "Pantry man."

The only way to be sure of catching all the ads for which you might qualify is to start at the beginning of the list of want ads and read them right down to the end. This sounds tedious, but it is worth the trouble, for you may see a job for which you are qualified, but which you had not considered before. Furthermore, an ad for a position outside your regular field of activity may indirectly lead you to a job. A man of 65, for example, who had just retired from a lifetime of work in the credit collection field, in scanning the want ads for some part-time work in which he could utilize his expertise, came across an ad for a telephone clerk with a local credit collection agency. Aware that he had too much experience for that particular job, he nevertheless called the agency. He described his experience and explained that he was not looking for a clerical job but for a position as a professional credit collection agent. An interview was arranged and a job at the salary and hours he wanted resulted. Had he not seen the ad under "Clerk," he would have missed this opportunity.

To take this technique one step further, contact all those concerns that you believe might employ persons in your line of work, even if the ads are for jobs completely different from what you want. Do not hesitate to approach employers. Most will be considerate and interested, and admire your initiative. This is often an effective way of landing a well-paying job.

Another thing to remember when answering want ads is to apply for any job that interests you even if you do not meet all the qualifications requested. Often the stated requirements are only meant as suggested levels of education and experience, and are not intended to rigidly exclude good applicants who do not meet them completely. Even in those cases where they are set as true minimum requirements, the employer could decide to reduce them to meet the existing job market should the ad's response turn out to be small. Therefore even if you only partially meet the qualifications called for, answer the ad and try your luck.

A word of caution in using the want ads. Unfortunately, there are some fast-buck operators who use the "Help Wanted" columns to sell false hope for earning extra income. Elderly people especially are sought out as targets for such deceptive advertising. They are promised excellent, and even spectacular profits, for easy spare-time work. But before the person can start collecting his profit, there usually is a catch, like an investment of money for inventory or the purchase of some necessary equipment. If you find that this type of ad interests you, investigate it carefully. Remember that a genuine offer can always stand some inquiry. Try checking with the Better Business Bureau, your banker, or your lawyer. If the offer is made by mail, you may write to the Chief Postal Inspector, U.S. Post Office Department, Washington, D.C. 20260, for information. Do find out particulars before you involve yourself.

PHONE TECHNIQUE

Ads in local newspapers often list a phone number to call. When applying over the telephone, be brief. Describe your most important qualifications and request an interview. Do not ask the salary or hours of work, or the like. Avoid discussing your age, or any controversial matters, but answer any questions directly and honestly. Your goal at this point is to get an interview. If the employer expresses doubt as to whether he could use you, do not let that deter you. Tell him that in any event you would appreciate an opportunity to speak with him. As long as he is willing to meet with you, do so. It will pay off. For even if he cannot hire you immediately, he will have an impression of you for some later date. Or he may recommend another employer for you to contact. Always follow up on such suggestions. When you contact the other employer and tell him you were recommended, it will carry some weight. Some of the best placements have had just such uncertain beginnings.

LETTERS OF APPLICATION

Looking for work in retirement is similar in many ways to finding a job at any time of life. For instance, one of the most effective methods is direct mail application. Armed with the list of firms gleaned from your research of the telephone directory, local newspapers, and related sources, select those that appear most promising or that interest you particularly. Send each a letter of application. Notice that I do not suggest that you send a résumé. At this point in your job search, a letter tailored to the individual company brings better results. While in the past the accepted practice was to submit a résumé at every turn, current experience has shown that a tailored letter is superior. One survey found 46 percent success in obtaining interviews with letters, versus only 2 percent by the use of the résumé.

Your letter of application should be brief. Use no more than one page, remembering that your prospective employer is a busy man. In one or two paragraphs describe what you consider to be your major work accomplishments and state the position you are seeking. Use standard business paper, not personal stationery, and have it typed neatly. Do not mention your age. In fact, avoid drawing attention to it in different ways, like specifying the number of years you worked. Instead, give only the figure for your experience in the work appropriate to the job at hand. Such phrases as "five years in a supervisory capacity" or "eight years in designing and marketing the product" could cover it. Describe in one sentence how you think you would be of value to the company. Write in a conversational tone, as though you were seated across the recipient's desk, talking to him. End the letter by requesting an interview. This is your objective—to get an appointment for a personal interview.

When writing your letter of application, give special attention to selecting the person to whom it will be addressed. Always send it to a specific individual, and the higher up in the company, the better, even the president. Never, never send a letter addressed in the company's name only, or simply to the "President," or "Director," or "Personnel Director." If you do, your letter will most likely be a waste of time and money. And make it a practice to stay away from personnel departments entirely. Too often the personnel director's assignment is to tell those who apply without a personal introduction that there are no jobs.

One of the simplest ways of finding out the name of the president or branch manager or any other company executive is to call the firm directly and ask. Tell the person who answers the phone that you are addressing a letter to the president (or branch manager) and would like to know his complete name and the proper spelling. You will get the information right off. If phoning is inconvenient, and if the company is of substantial size, a good source is the *Standard and Poor's Register of Corporations, Directors and Executives* or *Dun and Bradstreet Directory*. These publications, which are available in most libraries, contain the names of executives of all medium or large corporations in the United States.

While you may be well aware that the level of the position you are seeking does not warrant an interview with the company's president, do not for that reason alone write to a lower-level person. Even though you address your letter to him, the president most likely will never personally see it; indeed, his secretary will forward it to someone else. Fine. It will put you ahead of the game, for not only will your letter go to the person in the organization most likely to need your skills, but it will have been referred from the president's desk. That fact in itself guarantees that your letter will receive serious consideration.

Keep a list of the companies contacted as well as carbon copies of your letters. I suggest you send no more than ten letters at a time, for you want to be able to handle the interviews that result. If the first ten are well done, they may be all you will need. But do not be discouraged if you get a few negative replies or if some firms do not respond at all. You only need one job, and it will come if you persist.

Following are sample letters of application to help you in drafting your own:

Sample Letter of Application

                          1 Suburban Avenue
                          Capital City, Utah 73012
                          (Date)

Mr. Sam A. Jones, President
Utah Manufacturing Company
300 Broadway
Capital City, Utah 73015   Phone #

Dear Mr. Jones:

    An article in yesterday's *Journal-News* reports that your company has broken ground for a new plant. With this expansion of operations you may have need for a machinist with extensive experience.

    As machinist in the fabricating department of the Browning Company of Salt Lake City, I supervised an assistant machinist and four helpers. The Browning Company manufactures aircraft replacement parts.

    During the twelve years I worked for that firm I was promoted from helper to assistant, and then to head machinist. My work involved purchasing equipment, pricing job orders, and supervising the shipment of completed work.

    I am interested in obtaining employment locally. May I come in to speak with you? I would appreciate an opportunity to tell you more about my background.

                                        Sincerely,

                                        (signed)
                                        Paul Henry

Sample Letter of Application

> 54 Maybell Lane
> Waban, Massachusetts 03276
> (Date)

Mr. George Clarke, Manager
Bates Stenographic Service
625 Main Street
Boston, Massachusetts 06182

Dear Mr. Clarke:

I am writing to you in the hope that you have need for someone with extensive stenographic experience.

After more than a dozen years as a private secretary to the Vice President of the Massachusetts National Bank in Boston, I am currently seeking part-time employment.

My typing speed is 80 words a minute and my steno is 100 words a minute. I would like to work three days a week either at a business office or typing in my own home. I have an IBM Selectric typewriter available to me.

May I meet with you to show you examples of my work? Please write and let me know when it would be convenient for me to come in, or call me at P1–3–6432.

> Sincerely,
>
> (signed)
> Mrs. Mary Smith

Sample Letter of Application

1143 Lake Shore Drive
Chicago, Illinois 60606
(Date)

Mr. Jack Water, Plant Manager
Spartan Manufacturing Company
Chicago, Illinois 60606

Dear Mr. Water:

    Mr. Henry Brown of the Electrical Union told me that you will be hiring inspectors and assemblers. He also mentioned that you will be training new workers on-the-job.

    Although I have had no experience in assembly work, I do work well with my hands and enjoy doing work that requires manual dexterity and attention to detail. My favorite pastime is doing needlepoint. I often sell the items I make at the Main Street Arts and Crafts Store.

    I am anxious to obtain employment locally. The hours I can work are flexible and I would accept weekend and evening hours.

    I would appreciate an opportunity to demonstrate my ability. May I come in for an interview?

Respectfully yours,

(signed)
Mrs. Harriet Hochheimer
Phone 542–9123

THE INTERVIEW

Now for the interview. A good interview requires preparation. Try to learn as much as you can about the firm, and if possible, about the individual you are going to see. Find out how old the company is, its products or services, its size, projects the company is involved in or planning, the exact title of your interviewer, and his position in the company. A visit or call to your local library or chamber of commerce should supply the answers to these questions. Such books as *Thomas' Register of American Manufacturers, Moody's Industrial Manual, Poor's Register of Directors and Executives, Dun and Bradstreet's Middle Market and Million Dollar Directory* are good sources of information for medium to large companies. The data you gather will add to your confidence and help make your responses during the interview sound authoritative.

You should also review and study your complete history to refresh your memory of things you have done in the past that you may have forgotten. Think of how you will describe your qualifications and former job duties. Keep in mind two or three good reasons why you are interested in this particular job. The chances are excellent that you will be asked for your reasons. You may even want to jot down a few notes to which you can refer inconspicuously during the course of the interview. It will ensure that you cover all the points that you want to present.

A good idea is to bring to the interview a small card on which you have written down the important dates of your education and work history for help in filling out an application form. The usual application asks for:

1. Name and address of all employers you worked for, and the dates of your employment. You may be asked why you left each position, so think about it before the interview.

2. References. Names and addresses of at least two other persons who know of your abilities and background.

3. Names and addresses of all schools you attended, and the dates of graduation and type of diplomas received.

4. Subjects you took in college or special schools and number of credits received in major subjects.

5. Extracurricular activities at school, such as clubs and offices held.

6. Names of professional and service organizations to which you belong.

7. Social Security number.

It will help to have the above information readily available and not have to trust to memory. Having this information handy will ease the nuisance of filling out those application forms, which often are lengthy and detailed. Your speed in completing a long application may very possibly impress your prospective employer before the interview even begins. However, do not rush through the application. Be sure that you have answered all the questions properly and read it over before turning it in.

Write down the name and address of the company you are going to and the individual you will see, and take it with you to the interview. It is best not to rely on your memory. If you are unfamiliar with the area where the company is located, do not be embarrassed to phone beforehand for directions. If you cannot gauge accurately how much time the trip will take, travel the route before the appointed day to check it out. Such careful preparation will pay off in getting you to the interview on time and in a relaxed state. Of course you know to dress neatly and conservatively. But if your last job interview was 40 years ago, a few other reminders may be in order. Do not let your wife, husband, brother, or friend accompany you. Go to the interview alone. If you customarily wear glasses or a hearing aid, wear them to the interview. Dress appropriately for your age and the type of employment you are seeking.

During the interview, try not to be nervous, for anxiety can very easily ruin your chances. A nervous applicant gives the impression that he is not sure of himself or his qualifications for the job. An uneasy, anxious person is not in a position to do himself justice. Remember that you are being given the interview because the employer is interested in you. He had an opportunity to find out about you from your letter and he wants to talk with you. And you may be the most experienced person he has interviewed so far. When you first meet the employer, give him a good old-fashioned smile. It is impossible to smile and not relax.

Greet the interviewer by name as you enter. Shake hands, but only if the interviewer makes the first gesture. Take your cues from him. Do not smoke even if invited to unless you absolutely need to for composure. Look the interviewer directly in the eye. Be sincere and be yourself. Tell only those things about yourself that relate to the situation—your background, your experience. Don't waste the employer's time with trivial chatter but cover all the elements in your experience that are significant.

From the employer's standpoint, the most important thing about you is whether or not you can do the job. So do not bore or embarrass him with how badly you need work or how deserving a person you may be. Retired people are especially prone to this error. Some, who lack the courage of their convictions after long periods of inactivity, come across with the "hat in hands" approach. Don't do it. Don't apologize; don't brag; but don't be too modest either.

Be attentive and a good listener. Keep following the interviewer's lead. Do not answer by just saying yes or no. On the other hand do not talk too much and do not tell your troubles. Leave your troubles, anxieties, and self-pity at home. If you find yourself talking too long, give the lead back by saying, "Perhaps you have some other questions to ask me."

A few interviewers like to do most of the talking and judge you by your reactions. Others hardly speak at all. These are the hardest to deal with. Their attitude is that it is your job to sell yourself. This is your opportunity to cover all your good points. Discuss your qualifications as they relate to the particular company. Be careful not to make any slighting reference to any former employer, no matter how justified. This would appear to be an obvious point but there are many older applicants who do not appear to understand it. Blaming and complaining about former employers can only backfire. The interviewer will invariably jump to the conclusion, regardless of the explanation, that the applicant was at fault, not the former employer. He will assume that if you become his employee, you will be a chronic complainer. A better approach is to refer to the pleasant features about previous jobs. This gives the impression that your relationships in previous positions were all good and your interviewer is almost certain to conclude that you are the type of person who helps promote a pleasant atmosphere on the job. Since he wants cooperative employees, your chances for employment will be improved.

If the interviewer asks if you have any questions about the job, try to show interest in the firm and some enthusiasm for the position you are seeking. But be careful not to ask any questions which will make you appear overly particular, finicky, or doubtful of your ability to perform the duties. So ask questions carefully. If in doubt about the effect of your question, it is better to leave it unasked. If you want part-time work, be honest with the employer. Tell him how many hours you plan to work or what days are most convenient for you.

Handling the Question of Age. Should the subject of your age come up and the interviewer comment on it negatively, it would be appropriate to point out, not defensively but in a positive fashion, your good health, your vigor, etc. If possible, reply with factual statements, such as your excellent state of health as pronounced by your doctor. Stress your keen interest in being employed, your good work habits, and your skills. The results of studies of the work performance of older persons can be told to the employer. For example, tell him that older workers have better attendance and production records than younger workers. Their judgment and application to the job at hand has been shown to be greater. Many employers are pleased to learn these facts because they are unfamiliar with them. If your interviewer shows special interest, here are some other fact about the ability of older workers that you can tell him:

Studies of the University of Southern California's Gerontology Center have shown that the mental competence of healthy individuals remains at a high level beyond the age of 80.

A report by the Gerontological Society noted that workers between 60 and 75 can actually excel younger persons on the job because of their superior judgment, greater experience, and safe performance.

In a study of the performance of office workers by age groups, three important findings emerged. First, the differences in output per man hour are for the most part insignificant. Second, there is considerable variation among workers within age groups, so that large proportions of older workers exceed the average performance of younger ones. Third, workers in the older age categories had a steadier rate of output with considerably less variation from week to week than workers in the younger groups. These findings point to the advisability of evaluating workers on an individual basis, regardless of age.

Older workers are more strongly committed to the kind of work they do, and as a group they exhibit greater satisfaction with their jobs than younger workers.

You will find other points on the health and work performance of older workers in Chapter 1. But if the interviewer does not raise the question of your age, don't you.

Other Tough Questions. On the matter of salary, avoid the subject in the early part of the interview. Later, when you have learned something about the job and the employer has reached a conclusion regarding your potential value to his firm, you may want to discuss salary. Try to find out before the interview what similar jobs pay in your community and use that as a guide. Be realistic in the salary you ask, even if it is lower than what you are accustomed to receiving. Do not base your request on how much money you need but rather on your potential worth to the company.

If you are among those older persons, usually women, who have not had any recent work experience and the interviewer comments on this, respond that as a mature person you have had considerable life experience. Mention the activities you have participated in and the kinds of skills you have developed from them. For example, executive and secretarial skills are learned by participating in such organizations as parent-teachers associations, Boy or Girl Scouts, women's clubs, election campaigns, college and alumnae clubs, community agency boards. Style shows, writing publicity, reporting, amateur theatricals, and acting as program chairman are other activities which train persons in creative talents. Managerial skills are developed through organizing rummage sales, supervising church or club suppers, heading community chest or charity organization drives. Serving as volunteer nurse's aide, or handling child care duties, as well as all the other activities mentioned above, provide excellent practice in "how to handle people." Talents thus acquired are applicable to the fields of public relations, real estate sales, receptionist, news reporting, restaurant operation, product and service promotion, practical nursing, and social service.

Most interviews last between 20 and 30 minutes, so do not go on speaking endlessly. There is always the danger of talking yourself out of a job. Be alert to signs from the interviewer that the session is almost at an end. Be sure to thank him for the time and consideration given you, even if you feel discouraged about the results. If no job is immediately offered you, ask, "May I get in touch with you next week to find out if you have made a decision?" Or if there is no definite job opening for which you are being considered, ask if you might get in touch with him from time to time, because his company is one in which you are very much interested. And do not forget to do just that.

FOLLOW-UP

Follow-ups probably land far more jobs than do initial interviews. Your brief follow-up note should remind the interviewer of your talk. You can use these letters also to bring out points that you may have forgotten to cover in your interview. Express appreciation for the time given you and explain in as few words as possible your continued interest in the company.

Do not be too easily discouraged if an employer closes the interview with finality. Often those employers who give an applicant the feeling that there is little hope for a job are the ones finally impressed and turned around by the display of determination and persistence in an effective follow-up procedure. So plan periodic follow-ups by letter or telephone to any employer who has not given you a flat rejection and with whom you think a job possibility exists. Continue this every couple of weeks as long as the firm appears to be a "live" prospect.

80 [Help Yourself to a Job

Here are some sample follow-up letters:

Follow-up Letter

(Date)

Mr. James Klein, General Manager
American Chain Link Corporation
Suffern, New York 10934

Dear Mr. Klein:
   Thank you for taking the time to interview me last week.
   The description you gave of the duties and responsibilities of the position of office manager makes me more anxious than ever for the job. I believe that my past experience in a similar capacity with the United Hardware Company in New York City could be used to very good advantage in your organization.
   If there is any additional information you wish about my former work experience, please let me know. I would be happy to meet with you again to answer any additional questions. I look forward to hearing from you.

                                  Sincerely,

                                  (signed)
                                  George Hunt
                                  Address:
                                  Phone #:

Follow-up Letter

This letter adds some important information that was omitted at the interview:

(Date)

Mr. Jack Kurland, President
Kurland Chevrolet Company
Route 303
Nanuet, Mississippi 31267

Dear Mr. Kurland:
  Thank you for the opportunity you gave me last week to describe my qualifications for the vacancy of bookkeeper-typist.
  You expressed interest in the work I performed for the General Taxi Company in Rochester. I failed to mention that the name of my immediate supervisor was Mr. J. Scott Chamberlain. I worked directly for Mr. Chamberlain, who is chief dispatcher, for the full two years I was employed there. You may wish to speak with Mr. Chamberlain who has direct knowledge of my competency as a full-charge bookkeeper.
  I am most anxious to work for your organization because I know I could perform efficiently the duties you described. If there is any additional information you need, please let me know.

Sincerely,

(signed)
Mrs. Harriet Fuller
Address:
Phone #:

  If the interviewer suggests another company for you to contact, jot down the name immediately, checking out the spelling with him if necessary. If the address is not offered, do not press it. You can get the address from the telephone directory. Be sure to follow up such leads immediately. When you contact the suggested company, tell them who referred you. This is important. After the interview, analyze what happened and decide how you can make the next one better.

PREPARING YOUR RÉSUMÉ

The time to use a résumé is at the interview. The employer may ask for one, or you will want to leave one with him so he will have something tangible to refer to afterwards. Here are some important points to remember when designing your résumé. If possible, keep its length to only one page, two at the most. Remember, a résumé is not a complete personal history. It is only a synopsis, an outline. Do not include physical description, age, marital status, or salary. Do begin with that aspect of your qualifications that you consider your best feature. Usually this would be your most recent and highest level of work experience, but not necessarily. It might be your extracurricular activities, your educational achievements, or some special knowledge you possess. While it should be your best feature, it must also be relevant to the position for which you are applying.

Follow this with your other qualifications, such as other work experience, education, and community activities. You need not detail all your jobs, only those that bear on the work for which you are applying. Significant minor experience, if it relates to the job you are seeking, should be included. Note any promotion or recognition that has come your way as a result of success in a job. Be frank about your accomplishments, stating them briefly and factually. If you worked with special kinds of equipment, specify them. If you type or take shorthand, state the number of words per minute. For women who have not worked in some time, any experience, no matter how brief and whether paid or not, should be listed.

For schooling, you need only name your highest level achieved, but list principal subjects studied and any special courses. If you have been elected to professional societies in your field or if you belong to any wellknown service or social organizations, list them. If you have been recognized by awards or offices, mention them, too. Be sure to put your name, address, and telephone number at the top of the page. If you wish, you may indicate the job you are seeking at the beginning of the résumé.

In working up your résumé, try to make it interesting. Give it a little new twist, if possible, to take it out of the ordinary. Put yourself in the position of the prospective employer. Think of what you can tell him about yourself that will be impressive but at the same time factual. Do not include references. If and when the employer wants references, he will ask for them. Following are samples of résumés to guide you:

Sample Résumé

Richard A. Clifford
212 Washington Avenue
Blauvelt, New York 10964

Telephone 356-2112

Position Desired—Maintenance Man or Purchasing Agent (Two or Three Days a Week)

Working for only one employer, I have had quite varied experience.

As plant superintendent for the Haverstraw Chemical Company in Haverstraw, New York, I was in charge of plant operation and maintenance. This concern has an extensive facility which includes air conditioning, heating, and power generating equipment. When additional space was needed, I helped draw the specifications, design, and supervise the erection of the two new buildings. With the help of two maintenance men I was able to repair and maintain the entire premises without the need for any major replacements during the ten years I held this position. Furthermore the safety record at the plant consistently received commendations from the local chamber of commerce.

Previous to my assignment as plant superintendent, I worked in the purchasing, shipping, and personnel departments. In the purchasing department, I supervised the requisitioning of materials and supplies and had the authority to choose vendors for all equipment. My staff consisted of four shipping clerks and two office workers. My work in the personnel department involved interviewing applicants for technical positions and processing personnel records for the entire staff.

Education: Graduation from Peabody High School, Pittsburgh, Pennsylvania. One year at the Carnegie Institute of Technology where I took courses in chemical engineering.

Extracurricular activities: Organized the Industrial Management Club at the Haverstraw Chemical Company; president of the Board of Education of the North Passaic Central School District; treasurer of the Men's Club of the United Methodist Church; active in organizing the PTA at the local elementary school.

Sample Résumé

Anne R. Bradford
60 Broadway
Valley Cottage, New York 10936

Telephone: (914) 356–6342

Brief look at nearly 15 years in responsible administrative positions.
For the past seven years I worked for Shelling & Shelling of New Square, Inc. (personnel agency), in New Square, New York, as administrative assistant and executive secretary to the office manager. Besides secretarial duties, such as handling appointments, making travel arrangements, and greeting callers for my employer, I drafted my own replies to correspondence and performed library research on personnel subjects. I supervised a secretary and a typist who took

dictation and typed letters and reports for my employer and myself.

Before moving to this area, I was employed in Buffalo, New York, by the Mercantile Terminals, Inc., as office supervisor. My responsibility there was to handle all correspondence and contacts with manufacturers and their representatives who were our customers. Payroll and books of accounts, such as cash receipts, disbursements, and trial balance were under my supervision. I held that job for nearly five years, having been promoted from the position of supervisor of the secretarial pool of three stenographers and six typists. In that latter position, besides scheduling the work of my staff, resolving their technical problems, and reviewing their work, I was required to evaluate their performance, and interview and hire replacement staff.

My first job after college, which I held for four years, was with the Mercantile Terminals, Inc. at their headquarters in Cleveland, Ohio. I was stenographer to the president, relief switchboard operator, and assistant bookkeeper. My stenography is still in the 80 to 100 words-a-minute range and my typing is 60 words a minute.

Education: Graduation from Cleveland State University, *cum laude;* major in business administration. Secretarial course at Cleveland Business College.

Sample Résumé

Harriet J. Babbit
12 Mormon Drive
Salt Lake City, Utah 86571

Telephone: 515–9833

Position Desired: Promotional Assistant

Following are my major activities in the promotional and public relations field:
For three years I wrote a weekly column for the *San Jose*

Times, reporting on community meetings, such as women's clubs, church socials, Rotary and other service clubs. This required initiative in making contacts, and tact in maintaining good relationships with club directors. It also required the meeting of precise publishing deadlines.

As chairman of volunteers for District 5 of the March of Dimes in Salt Lake City for over four years, I recruited and trained more than 30 volunteers in fund-raising techniques. I supervised their activities on a daily basis, reviewing their reports and compiling them into a final annual report for headquarters. Each year we reached our fund-raising goal.

During the summer months while attending Hofstra College, I worked as public relations assistant for the Salt Lake City Young Women's Christian Association. I prepared leaflets and wrote newspaper releases highlighting each new program. I originated and supervised the preparation of a TV feature on our summer camp program. In recognition of my work, I was promoted to associate director. During the month-long vacation of the director, I had full charge of the public relations office.

As membership chairman of the Parent-Teachers' Association of Yorktown High School in Salt Lake City for two years, I directed drives that resulted in the doubling of total membership. As chairman of the scholarship fund committee, I helped screen applicants and participated in the selection of recipients. I spoke to the general meeting of the organization, describing our program, each year when I presented the award.

Education: Graduated from Hofstra University with a major in English. Recently completed two introductory courses, one in journalism and one in public relations techniques, at Salt Lake University.

6

GOOD LEADS FOR HARD TIMES

When business activity lags, finding a job is hard for everyone, skilled or unskilled, high-salaried or low, young or old. At such times, concerned job seekers watch and worry as the Help Wanted section of *The New York Times*, the bellwether of the employment market, shrinks. But we all know that in good times as well as bad there are always desirable jobs to be had. The question is how to find them. In this chapter the emphasis is on learning just that.

RECESSION BUSINESSES

Obviously, different businesses are affected in differing degrees by an economic recession. In fact, some lines of work may even benefit by a downturn in the economy. Which are they? Simply follow these thoughts for a moment.

When money is tight, the first things most families give up are luxuries, the "nice things" in life. Thus, while clothing is a necessity, new clothing may not be. Similarly new cars, new household appliances, new furniture, almost anything new becomes a luxury. Which just means that all kinds of repair services benefit—shoe repairing, private tailoring, cleaning and dyeing services, furniture refinishing, and so on. As one reweaving company executive put it, "When things are bad, alterations are good; when things are good, alterations are bad."

As people put off buying new automobiles and try to keep their old ones in good running condition, car repairs increase. Add to this the greater complexity of today's automobiles and the trend to mandatory vehicle inspection and pollution controls, and the auto parts industry booms. Analogously, people trying to stretch their dollars begin to do their own home maintenance, so do-it-yourself firms prosper, as do companies which serve the home-sewer.

Restaurants and entertainment firms suffer, but "fast food" establishments and the movies do well. The motion picture industry benefits because it offers a fairly inexpensive form of readily available mass entertainment. Even though incomes fall, leisure time may increase because of unemployment. But because they are unable to afford more expensive activities, consumers "buy down" by listening to music or watching a movie. They spend less on travel and seek entertainment closer to home. As they look for recreation they can afford, activities like bowling alleys (which have been called the poor man's country club) prosper. Camping and canoeing offer a simpler form of vacation, and equipment suppliers for these activities do a rushing business.

Retailers, wholesalers, and manufacturers of hobby materials and craft supplies for woodworking, weaving, pottery, ceramics, and other crafts do well. Hobbies offer an escape from the harsh realities of everyday living for persons with increased leisure and less money to spend. In addition, some collect stamps and coins, which grow in value, as a hedge against inflation. Others, who find gifts and home decorations priced beyond the limits of their budgets, make their own handcrafted items at considerable savings. And independent of a recession, and for that reason having a potential for continued growth, is the use of arts and crafts materials by such groups as the disabled, retirees, wounded veterans, and hospital patients. Doctors and psychiatrists now recognize the need for the creative use of enforced leisure hours, and hobbies are included in almost all programs for the elderly, handicapped, and the like.

Nurseries and garden supply businesses do well as homeowners grow vegetables and flowers as a relatively inexpensive recreation and to save on food bills.

During the 1930s book sales boomed, as they probably will whenever the economy falters. Readership of magazines and newspapers suffers, but books, besides being a source of entertainment, often provide advice and instruction as people find themselves facing new problems. Many persons opt for more education and book learning in their periods of idleness to fill the hours and to help improve their chances for finding work.

As bankruptcies develop, auctioneers and firms handling distress material become active, as do loan companies and credit collection agencies. All these fields are places for you to concentrate your job search. Many of them are particularly suited to the aptitudes of older persons. A recent want ad for a credit collection agency, for example, specifically called for a senior citizen to work part-time.

Health care is another occupational area in which many retirees find employment. Even in bad times, health care organizations retain their level of activity because the demand for such services is generally unrelated to the business cycle. If anything, periods of recession and substantial unemployment may increase the incidence of psychiatric and psychosomatic illnesses. Furthermore, Medicare, Medicaid, and private health insurance programs maintain the availability of funds. In fiscal 1974, government sources reported that only about $1 of each $3 spent for personal health care was paid out of pocket by the patient. Almost all the rest was paid by the government or private insurance, so that hospital and other health care often seemed "free" to recipients. Although many physical and dental check-ups were postponed, as well as cosmetic and elective surgery, the American Hospital Association found that the demand for hospital space remained high during fiscal 1974. The census in some suburban hospitals was down to 80 or 90 percent, but the large city institutions were still experiencing full-capacity use.

Private security is another field that prospers in a recession and in which many retirees find employment. Organizations which protect life and property are in demand as high unemployment rates foster more crime. There is also a general trend by Americans towards buying their own protection from crime. Private street patrol and private guard services, which were once the hallmarks of exclusive residential enclaves, are now used extensively by middle- and low-income residential areas as well as by business enterprises of all sizes. Everyone these days is security-conscious, and private guard firms and electronic detection services are benefiting.

If you investigate other new trends and fads, you will find businesses that will be putting on help even in a recession. The tennis business, for example, is good these days, as is the private aircraft field, which has benefited from the 55-mile-per-hour speed limit. Many salesmen, architects, and construction executives who must travel widely cannot afford the extra time traveling by automobile now entails and are taking to the air. Of course as a retiree you are not likely to want a job as a pilot or flight attendant, but remember that auxiliary departments of maintenance and management expand as the number of flights increases.

The current flow of large sums of money to the oil-producing countries has opened up many job opportunities in countries like Iran and Saudi Arabia. As these nations work to become more industrialized, they urgently seek the expertise of Americans. Retired military people, especially those who have technical know-how, are actively being recruited to go to that part of the world. Many of them, even in their senior years, are taking up the challenge.

JOB SKILLS NEEDED

Having indicated some of the businesses that prosper in bad times, let us turn to the types of skills that are needed by them. According to the results of a study of job vacancies made in early 1975, at a time when there was a marked reduction in the overall number of job openings, there was still a strong demand for qualified secretaries, stenographers, typists, and transcribing machine operators. The number of openings for such positions far outstripped the number of qualified individuals available to fill them. In the industrial field, there were shortages of applicants to fill vacancies for tool and die makers, machinists, automobile and maintenance mechanics, specialty cooks, executive housekeepers, and medical technicians. Openings for accountants, auditors, and insurance salesmen were also listed. At the same time, there was an oversupply of unskilled workers, receptionists, mail clerks, shipping clerks, and packers.

In a tightly competitive job market, those under 21 and those over 45 who have little education or few saleable skills find job hunting particularly discouraging. But personnel people report that even with the unemployment rate climbing, there is a pressing need in the business community for employees who are capable of doing quality work. It comes down to this. In any business climate, if you have a skill an employer needs, be assured your age will be secondary. Here are some illustrative cases:

After two years of retirement from his certified public accountant business, a 67-year-old man who found that he was having to pinch pennies, started to look for a job even though it was a recession period. He had no difficulty finding employment with a neighborhood chemical firm, where he was hired to fill an urgent need for a qualified part-time bookkeeper.

A 59-year-old draftsman who retired from both the Navy and NASA was quickly put to work reading electrical blueprints for a metal processing equipment manufacturer. Even though business was slow, his skill was needed.

A 64-year-old man, who had spent his whole working life in the administrative area of a trucking firm that left him without a pension, applied at one of the senior citizen employment offices. He was interviewed and given a typing test, which he passed with high marks, and was promptly put to work as a secretarial aide right there in the employment agency.

An 80-year-old man enrolled in a real estate class because he has a job waiting for him if he can pass the realtor's exam. His comments are worth repeating. "Where in the Bible does it say you should retire? Look how old Abraham was when he started a whole new nation. I've never felt like a rocking chair. I'd rather be an Abraham that starts off over the hills looking for something new."

Finally, remember that labor shortages generally develop in areas where young workers are reluctant to accept positions in which career opportunities are limited, where jobs lack status and prestige, or in which the industry's overall activity is decreasing. Retirees, not interested in struggling up a new career ladder, can take advantage of this by applying in areas that are less attractive to younger workers. Agriculture, apparel manufacturing, railroads, and laundry service are such fields. These industries report a higher than average proportion of older workers. Government employment and the clerical fields also show a large proportion of older workers. In these latter areas, the lack of prestige generally associated with such employment apparently accounts for their low appeal to younger workers.

PART-TIME WORK

An effect of bad times that works to the advantage of retirees looking for work is the overall increase in the number of part-time jobs. As business slows down, employers start to substitute part-time for full-time help. As they become more vigilant of expenditures, they attempt to cover peak-load periods without a commitment to large staffs, with the result that they hire more part-time and temporary help than usual.

As a rule, part-time or casual work is shunned by younger workers who need full-time wages. Such jobs thus become available to older persons, for whom a part-time job is ideal because of the Social Security restriction which limits the amount of money they may earn. Social Security Administration records show that less than 40 percent of working men over the age of 65 hold full-time jobs. In order to stay within the Social Security ceiling of $2,760 a year (effective January 1, 1976), retirees can work only about 24 hours a week at the minimum wage and fewer hours at higher rates of pay. Also, some retirees seek part-time employment as a testing ground to see whether they can cope with the demands of full-time employment and to give themselves confidence to do more.

If you are looking for part-time work, here are places where you may find it. Part-time work is more likely to be available in service than in industrial and commercial areas. Tourist agencies, churches, schools, libraries, hospitals, catering firms, department stores, hotels, restaurants, professional offices, cleaners, filling stations, amusement parks, theaters, and nurseries are just a few of the types of organizations that perform services for others. Finance, insurance, and real estate are service industries that have experienced rapid growth in recent years and which employ a relatively high proportion of older workers. Fortunately for the elderly, the service sector of our economy as a whole is expected to continue to increase in proportion to other areas, so it will remain an important source of job opportunities.

In the retail trade, temporary and part-time help has always been common. Sales-clerking work can usually be obtained for less than a full week because extra help is always needed for peak hours, in the evening, and on Saturdays. Jobs in addition to selling which older people can perform well and which are often available on a part-time basis are handling merchandise, stocking shelves, and taking inventory. Older women especially should consider the retail field since it has always employed a high proportion of them.

Part-time employment is often available in businesses which have several work shifts and in which broken schedules or regular peak-load periods occur in the normal course of doing business. Banks and other financial institutions, for example, have cashier and teller jobs commonly available on a part-time basis. Temporary and seasonal work is often found in businesses that have definite "peak" seasons. For accountants, there is income tax time; for department stores, the Christmas shopping days; and for travel agencies, the summer vacation months. In the summer months, also, resort hotels, parks, beaches, camps, and restaurants in vacation areas need additional help. In Cape Cod, Massachusetts, a popular retirement area, its elderly residents are making solid inroads into the summer resort job market there. Restaurants and hotel managers have found that older persons perform very well as desk clerks, bellhops, and chambermaids, jobs which in the past had been the domain of vacationing youths. Now the employers heap praise on the elderly. One said, "They are willing to work hard and accept responsibility, not like the kids who just want to make a few dollars so they can take off." The enthusiasm is shared by the retirees. One man who is working as a busboy in a large Hyannis restaurant said, "I retired about four years ago and found I was going out of my mind. I always worked with my hands and with people, so this job suits me perfect. Besides, I can use the money."

During the winter season, Florida experiences an influx of tourists and part-time jobs become available in all sorts of activities. In Al Lang Field, the ball park in St. Petersburg, spectators are a bit surprised when they are escorted to their seats by a staff of ushers ranging in age from 56 to 84. They are all retired people who get paid $5 a day plus tips during game time.

Large industrial companies hire few part-time employees, not because of their retirement plans, for these rules ordinarily do not apply to part-time or temporary workers, but because they are not organized to handle the special clerical procedures which would need to be set up. The costs of these, plus the training of new workers, additional health insurance premiums, and social security deductions discourage them from hiring part-time help. Similarly, our governmental jurisdictions use few part-time workers as they find the coming and going at odd hours and the additional paperwork undesirable.

Exceptions to this negative attitude are developing as industrial psychologists search for ways of increasing efficiency by altering the monotony of regular work. In some cases the use of part-time positions has been proposed as a solution. The city of Berkeley in California is examining a job restructuring program which would allow city employees the option of working a 20-hour workweek or 6 months out of the full year. Such a program, if adopted, could open more opportunities for the employment of senior citizens.

FIRMS THAT HIRE THE ELDERLY

As the image of the older person improves and more retirees return to work and demonstrate their ability, some employers are coming around to the idea that they actually prefer to employ persons over 65. If you are finding job hunting difficult because of a business recession, let me acquaint you with employers who will welcome your application.

At Fertl, Inc., a small company on Marshall Street in South Norwalk, Connecticut, that produces starter material for garden plants, the average age of the employees is 68. The company's only product is a packet of small cubes made from potting soil, moisture retainers, and nutrients, each containing several vegetable or flower seeds. Founded in 1956 by Hoyt Catlin when he was 65, the business did not start out with the idea of hiring older people, but just developed that way. Mr. Catlin attributes the company's success to the sixteen fine employees, all in their 60s, 70s, 80s, and 90s. His work force, he believes, has less absenteeism and employee turnover than any firm its size. Some employees work short schedules, but others put in longer days than people half their age. A few of the current employees were placed there by the Senior Personnel Placement Bureau of Norwalk, Connecticut, one of the senior citizens employment services listed in Appendix B. Mr. Catlin has said, "A substantial part of the success of Fertl is contributed by the quiet atmosphere in our factory and the grace with which our senior men and women approach their daily tasks. Sometimes they sing during their coffee breaks, off-key a little bit, not much harmonizing, corny, of course, but it sounds great to me, and I hope it continues."

The Texas Refinery Corporation, TRC for short, at 840 North Main Street, Fort Worth, Texas, is a much larger firm that favors the elderly. A manufacturer of roofing, wall coatings, and paints, TRC markets its products only through direct selling. Distribution is nationwide and there are offices and refineries even in such far-off places as Moose Jaw, Canada; Mexico; and the Duchy of Luxembourg. One-fifth of their salesforce are men over 60. The company president confesses that it is not a charitable thing he is doing, but rather that he finds employing men of senior years just good business. The highest sales averages are often turned in by those over 60. The folksy, low-key approach used by the older salesmen seems to work especially well for TRC's products. The arrangement works out well for the older salesmen, too;

many earn high wages. They have organized themselves into a club called the "Sizzling Sixties," whose president describes it as "an organization of men who are still young enough to dream, and to make those dreams come true."

Former selling experience is not a requirement to work for TRC. Farmers, mechanics, government workers, construction workers, professional men, retired military, and former owners of small businesses are among those who have been employed. An older salesman may work full-time or part-time (if he wishes to keep his earnings within Social Security limitations, for example). With no formal training program and with little or no direct supervision, the salesmen have the freedom of independent contractors. As one septuagenarian puts it, "For 4 hours a day, I'm as good a man as I ever was. But after that, I want to take a nap and recoup. With this job, I can work mornings, and then call it a day. It's perfect for a man of my age."

SELLING OCCUPATIONS

The selling field as a whole is an effective vehicle for post-retirement employment. Many retirees who have never sold before have made a successful second career out of selling. The maturity, integrity, and stability of older persons are particular assets in direct selling. Retirees go into this field because they like the independence it allows them. With no time clock to punch, they can set their own hours and limit their incomes if they wish to stay within the social security limit. The opportunity for meeting new people is an added perquisite they enjoy.

In choosing a selling career, select a product or service which has some special meaning for you. A camera bug, for example, might do well selling photographic equipment. A former housewife and mother could be successful with children's furniture. Whatever product you choose, make sure the company you will represent has a good reputation. Check it out with your bank, chamber of commerce, or Better Business Bureau.

Selling real estate works out especially well for older

people, since age apparently has its advantages in that field. The patience and diligence of most older persons evokes the trust of prospective customers. Particularly in selling to young marrieds, an older person as a "father" figure can be quite successful. However, as in all selling, your achievements will be in direct proportion to the energy, ability, initiative, and perhaps knack, you exhibit. Since licensing of realtors is mandatory in most states, you will have to pass a written examination in the fundamentals of real estate and relevant state laws. To prepare yourself, you can easily locate schools in your area which teach courses in real estate. Real estate selling is a field in which women as well as men do well; in fact, about one-third of the participants are women. However, a word of advice to those who do not like detail. There is heavy paperwork involved in real estate—bills of sale, mortgages, insurance, and so forth. Caution should also be exercised in entering this field in bad times when the real estate market is often depressed. At such times be sure to investigate the potential in your area first, observing the market and discussing it with individuals in the field. Current records of real estate deals show that sales of high-priced homes remain constant despite the recession. Apparently upper-income Americans in many areas still have the resources needed to buy expensive homes, so gear your selling efforts accordingly.

Another area in which older persons do well is automobile sales, because a customer who plans to spend several thousand dollars for a car wants to deal with someone who is mature and reliable. These jobs are available on a part-time basis and often do attract retirees. So if you know a bit about cars, make a good appearance (possess an honest face), have confidence and perseverance, plus the ability to speak clearly and persuasively, this could be just the job for you. Of course, in a business recession direct your efforts to the used car market, for new cars sell poorly, except for high-priced cars which, like expensive homes, continue to be bought.

In contrast to other forms of direct selling, the insurance field is a complicated business, with options, waivers, riders, and other legal terminology. But here again your age can be a tremendous advantage, as an older person is more able to inspire confidence in others. Success in the insurance field also requires an outgoing personality and the ability to meet and befriend people. Part-time work is customary, though appointments may require evening and Sunday hours. A license to sell insurance requires a written examination, which means a lot of time and learning on your part if you have no previous background in the field. But if you qualify, you will find that here, as in other independent selling jobs, your earnings will reflect the initiative and hard work that goes into it. That is exactly what makes selling jobs so attractive in recession days to older persons, who know what it means to apply themselves and work hard.

PROFESSIONAL FIELDS

Teaching. One of the best examples of an organization which has prospered through the hiring of retirees is the Hastings College of Law of the University of California at San Francisco, which in 1948 began hiring law professors and prominent lawyers who had been involuntarily retired from their jobs elsewhere. In the years since, Hastings College has grown to become the largest law school west of St. Louis, with one of the highest records of alumni achievement in the nation. Today over half of the faculty is made up of former retirees.

In a recent poll taken among the students of Hastings College, the man chosen "Professor of the Year" was not a young teacher with whom "they could identify," but a distinguished scholar who had passed his 83rd birthday! And the professor who received the next highest honor, "Outstanding Lecturer of the Full-Time Faculty," was also an octogenarian. These honors attest to the continued ability of older persons to perform well in their chosen profession. Here are some student comments about other members of the faculty, all over 65: "He is probably the most outstanding professor I have ever had." "Pearls of wisdom just flow from the master's mouth." "He is an educator in every sense of the word." "We rate him near-perfect."

The extent to which the teaching field might be a way to utilize the older professional was investigated by the General Electric Company in a survey which queried G.E.'s professional employees about their interest in an academic life in the retirement years. More than half (54 percent) were interested. Of the colleges asked to indicate their interest in utilizing this type of personnel, 94.4 percent said they were. But most pointed out that retirement from regular employment and transfer to their institutions before the age of 65 would be essential if these individuals were to be of any real value to the colleges.

A study by the National Science Foundation seems to confirm that an early start is necessary for a successful academic second career. It was found that retired military officers were effective teachers of mathematics and science in secondary schools. Since the military retire at a younger age than most industrial professionals, their earlier start was believed to facilitate their successful transfer into teaching. It is important for professionals interested in an academic post-retirement career to investigate its potential early in their senior years.

Consulting Work. Another approach which has effectively helped professionals bridge the gap from full-time employment to part-time retirement is consulting work. Numerous lawyers, engineers, economists, and other professionals, as well as top executives, have negotiated consulting contract arrangements with their employers to enable them to work exclusively for them in retirement. In this way a former employee becomes a private employer. He assumes all the costs of fringe benefits and is no longer bound by established mandatory retirement rules. An interesting example of this kind of employment is the one worked out by a grand old man of 92. Officially retired in 1966 from the position of plant manufacturing supervisor, he still reports to his former pharmaceutical employer every time a batch of cough syrup is made up. On some occasions, he will even walk the mile and a quarter distance to reach the factory, attesting to his continued vigor. His skill is so phenomenal, his employer believes him to be virtually irreplaceable. He is under a consulting contract which provides a monthly income for the rest of his life. In return, the firm has the privilege of calling on him for advice whenever it is needed.

As desirable as such a setup may be, consulting arrangements with former employers are not always possible, as not all firms are geared for this type of operation. For example, a pharmacist was being retired at 65 from his job as director of the nursing home division with a major hospital and institutional supply company. His immediate supervisor was most anxious to retain his expert services, and a mutually acceptable contractual arrangement, setting forth hours of work, rate of pay, duration, etc., was worked out between them. But when it was presented to top brass for approval it was turned down on the grounds that there was no precedent for such action in the company. Because they had no personal knowledge of the pharmacist's expertise, management refused to make an exception for him. Disappointed, he left the firm to seek work elsewhere.

When a consulting arrangement with a former employer does not work out, give consideration to establishing a consulting firm of your own. For professionals who were able to develop a number of personal business contacts during their former employment, such action could be quite lucrative. An outstanding example is the chief geologist of the Exxon Oil Company, who was retired at 65. Still full of energy, he set up shop as an oil consultant with the full knowledge and permission of his former employer. Today at 81, he is decidedly unretired and a centimillionaire. His successful oil finds for several Australian-based companies are producing high royalties for himself and his future heirs.

Besides starting your own consulting business, there is the additional possibility of joining an established consulting firm in your field. The telephone yellow pages can help locate those in your community. Working for someone else has its advantages. Here is an illustration: A gentleman who retired from a position as vice president in charge of the investment management division of a major New York bank contemplated opening his own investment advisory service in his hometown, suburban community in order to avoid commuting. He decided to discard the idea, however, and took a position with a small but well-established investment advisory service in New York City. He realized that to do a good job in his field, he needed to be where the action was. Furthermore, his new employer had ready contacts which would enable him to generate immediate income for himself.

Consulting work would be appropriate for either a white-collar or blue-collar worker, provided he has some very special skill in a trade or profession. Those who do should very seriously consider using this skill before looking for any other kind of work. As with part-time work, the call for consultants increases as the economy softens, because employers prefer the flexibility it gives them in contrast to adding the needed skilled workers to their permanent staff.

There are some groups of retirees who have banded together to offer their pooled skills on a contractual basis to local businesses and government. One such organization is Experience, Inc., of Hemet, California, which came into being as the result of a study made in 1967. At the request of the mayor of Hemet, a Committee for Productive Retirement was formed. The committee studied the problem, formed a membership organization, and recruited senior citizens with many kinds of skills and talents. The organization set as its operating objective to offer research, planning, and advisory services under a contractual arrangement. On its staff now are seniors with specialty skills which are not readily available in the area. When projects are obtained, individuals with the necessary skills are assembled as a team. Examples of the projects handled are a land-use survey, new product evaluation and a custom drafting presentation.

A group with strong community backing is the Mohawk Development Service in Schenectady, New York, which was organized to find continuing employment for engineers and other technical personnel retired by the General Electric Company and the American Locomotive Company, both of that city. The service was designed to provide work for those who were unhappy in retirement, or who needed the income. It offers engineering and drafting help to local companies. A good deal of its business has come from contracts with General Electric in such important projects as the Knolls Atomic Power Laboratory, where a number of the group worked continuously for several years. In a period of nine years, Mohawk is reported to have employed 125 people and paid salaries of $828,000.

Less formally organized groups are operating in many communities. The Older Adult Community Action Program, 6509 Delmar Boulevard, St. Louis, Missouri 63130, for example, is working to enlist individuals in the skilled trades and professions in that area. To locate a group in your own community, check your chamber of commerce or local retirement organization. If there is none, why not consider starting a talent pool of retirees yourself. Carpenters, machine shop and metal workers, accountants, public relations experts, and others could combine to offer their services. If you accept small jobs that regular commercial firms so often refuse to handle, you will undoubtedly be very busy.

SHELTERED WORKSHOPS

Sheltered workshops are another source of jobs for retirees. They have been in use for some time now in England where pensioner workshops have been set up by companies to utilize the skills and experience of retirees. Rolls Royce, for instance, maintains one where retired employees work up a prototype, custom build, and repair or do other special jobs inconvenient to the mechanized output of the parent company. In America, sheltered workshops are being established by non-profit or charitable institutions in order to employ individuals unable to meet the demands of the ordinary workplace. Simple assembly, inspection, and repair jobs are commonly performed on contract from local businesses. Employment is most often on a part-time or temporary basis, though sometimes full-time work is also available. Because the skills required are minimal, the wage rates are quite low. However, the sheltered workshops are invaluable for older people who need to learn new skills because of changing capacities, or those who have become discouraged by long periods of idleness and unsuccessful job hunting. The relaxed, unpressured atmosphere of these workshops often gives workers renewed confidence in their abilities.

As indicated in Chapter 4, some senior citizen employment services operate sheltered workshops. The Jewish Vocational Service in East Orange, New Jersey (67 North Clinton Street), for example, maintains a Work Center on Aging. They train older people who have been forcibly retired or who have obsolete or no skills, and then refer them to appropriate regular jobs. Senior citizens ranging in age from 55 to 86 are currently in the program. The workshop is also used to employ the disabled on an extended basis. For information on sheltered workshops in your area, write the Association of Rehabilitation Facilities, 5530 Wisconsin Avenue, Washington, D.C. 20015.

SKILLED TRADES

Workers in the skilled trades obtain employment in business and industry predominantly through their unions. Fortunately for the elderly, some unions are actively resisting the forcible retirement of their members and working hard to keep them employed. The building trades has effected the inclusion of a clause in many employer contracts requiring the hiring of a number of workers over a given age on each project. The International Brotherhood of Electrical Workers (IBEW), for example, recommends the following provision to its locals: "On all jobs requiring seven (7) or more journeymen, if available every seventh (7th) man shall be 60 years of age or older." Practically every contract negotiated in the construction industry has such a provision, though the number of journeymen and the age requirement, which in some cases is as low as 50, varies. Retired or semi-retired skilled tradesmen who wish to continue working at the union wage in industry should check with their respective unions to see what their rights are under their contracts. Some agreements have the undesirable feature of requiring the forfeiture of a portion of one's pension under certain conditions of re-employment.

While the construction industry has been severely hurt by the recession, other skilled trades have fared better. The bakery union, for example, reports a good demand for skilled bakers. Older men are advised to concentrate on small bakeries, where much of the work is handcrafted and the need for skill greater.

HIRE YOURSELF

Every American has at some time in his life dreamed of owning his own business where he would have the freedom to exercise his initiative and reap direct rewards from his efforts. Many persons on retirement feel that at last they can indulge in that long-standing wish. But self-employment is not for everyone. It requires initiative and energy because the owner of a small business must be a self-starter and a jack-of-all-trades. He must be able to analyze the market, arrange for financing and be a promoter and salesman. For those who can handle it, self-employment can be most rewarding both financially and in personal satisfaction.

Some may think that a business recession is no time to start a new venture, but if you have a skill and the business sense to go with it, you can prosper. For encouragement, let me tell you that a survey by the National Association of Manufacturers found that persons over 65 who start their own small businesses are considerably more likely to succeed than younger men. And here are a couple of success stories:

Dave G. at 75 is the "Mr. Fixit" of his community in a New York City suburb. Serving a clientele of many satisfied customers, he has been in this business with the aid of his wife, for ten years. She acts as salesperson; he does the work. In his former occupation as a commercial photographer he developed the patience that he needs in his new work. He specializes in lamp repair and even hires extra hands occasionally to help him.

Leo J. W. retired from an insurance agent job but could not sit still. He describes his feelings this way. "You go crazy. For me, I could not sit, could not eat, could not sleep. I was getting tired, sick, and nervous. I have to do something.

Doing nothing is no good." He heard that air cargo was a profitable business but that few people were in it. The idea intrigued him, and despite the fact that he hated to fly and had never flown, he decided to investigate, flying around the world to do so. He attended schools of different airplane manufacturers, went out on the ramps and watched how cargos were loaded, asked questions, talked with international shipping firms, learned rates, airport problems, fees. He believes that he absorbed 20 years of experience in the three-and-a-half years he spent learning the business. He was convinced money was to be made in air cargo. Now the owner of two jet engine planes, he maintains six crews, regularly travels around the world to pick up contracts, and is a very busy man indeed.

Careful planning and preparation are needed to succeed, and financial reserves may be needed to carry you through the often lean start-up time of a new venture. So be cautious, but do strike out on your own if you have the determination. Let me suggest some possible small businesses.

A skilled trade lends itself quite readily to small business operation. Many individuals skilled in plumbing, electrical work, carpentry, auto mechanics, and television repair go out on their own to keep busy in retirement. But other skills can be used in the same way. If you are a skilled bookkeeper, you can offer a tax and bookkeeping service to local businesses. A skilled office worker could develop a clerical service, doing mailing, typing, and mimeographing for small firms. Those experienced in tailoring or home sewing could operate as an individual entrepreneur or even open an instructional center. A knitting or cooking school is an idea for an enterprising former housewife. Even a hobby could be made to pay in a small business of your own. When Jack C. and his partner Jack T. retired, they turned their carpentry hobbies into a profitable craftsman shop, producing custom-designed handcrafted furniture that resembles its 18th-century counterpart right down to the wooden pegs. They also restore and repair antiques. Together they converted an old concrete-block gas station in Florida into a combination workshop and adjoining gift store, run by one of the wives. Both men consider themselves retired. "And we're thinking of taking Mondays off to prove it," announces Mr. T. A retired woman in San Francisco became so interested in searching for a 1909 Lincoln penny worth $150, which she finally found, that she turned her coin-collecting hobby into a business. She opened a small coin shop and is having a grand time while also earning money.

What small businesses are right for you as a retiree if you have no special skills or appropriate hobbies? Some possibilities are cigar or refreshment stand, retail store, vending machine route, parking lot, laundromat, chauffeuring, delivery or shopping service. Opening a small store and selling a product which he knows about is a popular business venture for a retired person. A retired professor of literature has made a success out of a small bookstore, for example, and a housewife who had done extensive home sewing opened a local fabric store and prospered.

If a retail outlet appeals to you, be sure to analyze carefully whether there is sufficient demand for your product or service where you plan to locate. The regional office of the Small Business Administration and your banker can help with advice on this aspect and on related problems, helping to prevent costly mistakes. The Small Business Administration can also lend money to small businesses if money is unobtainable elsewhere, but about half of the total funds required will have to come from your own resources. The Internal Revenue Service has booklets which will help with the bookkeeping aspects of your business. Available free of charge at your local IRS office is a "Tax Guide for Small Businesses," "Record Keeping for the Small Business," "Tax Information on Operating a Business in Your Home." The Service Corps of Retired Executives (SCORE), a volunteer organization which helps small businesses that need managerial and technical operating assistance, is also available in many areas to help with problems as they arise. If you cannot locate offices of these organizations in your local phone book, a letter addressed to any of them and sent to Washington, D.C., will reach its destination. The National Association of Accountants, working closely with the Small Business Administration and the Office of Minority Business Enterprise of the U.S. Department of Commerce, has developed a program to help needy small businessmen and women get started in the right direction. NAA member volunteers offer free confidential accounting and other financial and management advice. Write to the National Association of Accountants, Socio-Economic Program, 919 Third Avenue, New York, N.Y. 10022.

One drawback to opening a small store is the substantial financial investment needed for equipment, rental, insurance, and merchandise. Even if the plan is to start small, at least $20,000 is needed. As an alternative to the ordinary store, the commission retail shop is a good one for older men and women to consider. Here the proprietor does not purchase the merchandise he sells but takes goods on consignment, collecting a commission on the sale. Less capital is required than in the standard retail establishment because there is no outlay for inventory, and usually neither heavy equipment nor skilled employees are needed. This type of business is often run successfully on a part-time basis and even out of one's home or garage. It is more personal, relaxed, and casual than other types of stores, and is appropriate for the sale of arts and crafts, antiques, handmade furniture and clothing, or used goods.

In this same category are mini-flea markets or swap-and-shop stores that are currently in vogue in suburbia. These are leisurely operations that can be kept small and are well suited to the capabilities of elderly proprietors. Today's emphasis on saving pennies and the conservation of resources has made these used-goods establishments popular.

The motel business is one that I do not recommend for older persons. Many retirees envision the operation of a motel as leisurely and profitable, but as a rule even a small motel requires more stamina and capital than most retirees have. It is not a job for the average retired or semi-retired person.

A vending machine route, on the other hand, is quite suitable for an older person. The choice of operation is vast. Everything from food to clean clothes, a shoeshine to a photograph, is available today by dropping a few coins into a machine. Vending machine operators buy the machines, find locations for them, keep them in repair, fill them with merchandise, and collect the coins. Theft will be one of your major problems since vending machines are prime targets for vandals and petty thieves. If a vending route sounds good to you, you may want to consider a vending franchise which will provide you with an established territory. Be careful, however, when entering into such an arrangement. High-pressure promoters often victimize older people by promising them profitable routes in exchange for the purchase of the machines. Once the equipment is sold, the routes sometimes turn out to be unprofitable, or non-exclusive territory. So investigate fully before you involve yourself.

FRANCHISE OPERATION

Many kinds of operations are franchised today. Some of those appropriate for older persons are drive-in dairies, temporary help agencies, craft shops, paint stores, soft drink stands, doughnut shops, sports and recreation establishments, shoe repair shops, car washes, travel agencies, cosmetics and health aids, mail order items, lawn care supplies, home maintenance services, building and auto products and services, auto rentals, TV, newspaper, and many more.

The franchising method means simply that a large national organization sells a local businessman the right to run the business under the organization's name and to use its methods. Franchising has been a part of the American economy for years, but it has recently experienced enormous growth. In a business recession, when it takes more expertise to succeed, franchising is an especially desirable arrangement. It provides a small investor with the opportunity to become self-employed with a reduced risk of failure. Reduced, that is, not eliminated, for success is not guaranteed, and your income will depend on your efficiency in operating the business. But you will have the advantage of operating under a successful corporate name which is advertised nationally, and you will receive training and management assistance from experienced personnel. As a franchisee in an established business, you may be able to avoid the long dry period just after opening, because a considerable amount of trial and error is eliminated. But you will pay for this advantage in the form of a percentage of the profits, a franchising fee, or an arrangement which requires you to buy all products or equipment exclusively from the franchisor.

Some franchising operations require sizable capital investment and hard work, though others need less money and time. For the majority, an investment of from $5,000 to $20,000 is expected. Your capital outlay will be less, generally speaking, in a franchise operation than in going into business completely on your own. Furthermore, it is often possible to borrow some of the money from the franchisor himself, whose credit facilities can be a great help in a tight money market.

Unfortunately, the rapid growth of franchising has attracted a number of unprincipled operators. Charges of exaggerated promotions have involved franchisors of motor oils and other auto supplies, light manufacturing, swimming pools, and rug cleaning equipment. As a prospective franchisee, it is important that you carefully examine the arrangement before becoming legally liable. Here are some general rules to follow: Stick to the mainstream of franchising and seek out the best franchising opportunities in your field of interest. A comprehensive list is given in the annual *Directory of Franchising Organizations*, available in most libraries. Check the reputation of the franchisor with the Better Business Bureau, and if the offer is made by mail, with the Chief Postal Inspector, U.S. Post Office Department, Washington, D. C. 20260.

If the franchisor is well known, has a good reputation and a successful franchising operation, you can proceed with confidence. Still, investigate further. Find out everything you can about the operation, the training and management assistance offered, the advertising programs conducted, and particularly about the profits you can expect. Ask to see certified figures of franchisees operating at your anticipated level of activity and then visit some of these franchises. By personal contact you can view all aspects of the operation and question the proprietors on such things as services, equipment, advertising, and profits. Check the terms of your agreement carefully. Who buys the supplies, who chooses the location, and is it leased from the company? Will you be protected from rival franchise companies? How many hours will you be expected to work and will you need to hire employees? Are you free to sell the franchise? Be suspicious of exaggerated advertising appeals, initial fees that are excessive in proportion to sales volume, too high costs of initial equipment, and agreements that do not give to you the power to make basic decisions. While you are making your investigation, legitimate franchising concerns will also investigate you. Beware of any company that is not selective of its franchisees, or which engages in such high-pressure tactics as insisting on a quick signature to save a "territory" for you, without checking you out. After you have satisfied yourself about the franchisor, you will still need a lawyer to negotiate the final agreement and examine the fine legal points.

COTTAGE INDUSTRY

For those confined to their homes because of a physical disability, or those who need or want to work out of their homes for any reason, there are still innumerable opportunities for remunerative work. A "cottage industry," which is what a business operated out of one's own home is called, has several advantages. First, your capital outlay will be small because there is little or no investment in office space, furnishings, or retail facilities. Second, your equipment needs will be minimal and you will probably not have any employees and employee problems. Third, there are no transportation worries in bad weather. However, because your home is your office you will need an extra measure of self-discipline to set working hours and keep to them. There are always a great many distractions at home, and the urge to procrastinate in favor of more pleasurable tasks can mean a constant battle with one's conscience.

There are unlimited ways to work out of your home, including the obvious field of arts and crafts. Those with a special talent, skill, or hobby are particularly fortunate. Here are two examples of skills paying off in a home business.

Lucy Geist at 88 is still turning out the Lucy doll to the delight of thousands of little girls. The foot-high rag dolls are made entirely by hand, and perhaps what makes them so special is the tender loving care and pride of workmanship Mrs. Geist puts into each one. Fifteen years ago Mrs. Geist received a commission from the U. S. Military Academy to dress dolls in their military museum. Having completed the task she has not yet found time to visit the exhibit. "Too busy," she says. Last year she made 650 dolls and regularly has a six-month backlog of orders.

Marion J. began baking bread 20 years ago more for her own amusement than anything else. Today she is known as "the bread lady" and has a lucrative business operating out of her farmhouse kitchen. Her baked goods are free of chemicals and preservatives and she thus has a ready market in the growing number of natural food fanciers.

In some areas groups have organized retail outlets to sell arts and crafts produced at home by older men and women. The New York Elder Craftsman Shop at 850 Lexington Avenue, New York City 10021, is one. It sells the work of men and women over 60 from all over the country and returns to each a high percentage of the retail price. Another is the flourishing Northwest Senior Craftsmen, second level of Pier 70, Box # 32, Seattle, Washington 98109. No doubt you can locate similar shops in your vicinity.

If you are not artistically inclined, perhaps your former job can be adapted to working at home. A former secretary could do typing of manuscripts, playscripts, and term papers. A notice on the bulletin board of the nearest college or an ad in a writer's magazine would surely bring plenty of orders. A former office worker could start a telephone answering service for doctors, dentists, or other professionals, or small businessmen who do not have full-time help. Or consider a reminder service to alert people of appointments, birthdays, etc., and to make travel arrangements and reservations for them. This service could be sold to business executives and affluent housewives. Or visit local stores and offer to phone a list of their customers to inform them of a special sale or other event for a fee. Also, all kinds of products can be sold by phone. Many retirees who have trouble getting around try this. However, they often find such work tedious and low paying, but it is readily available. The classified section of your newspaper will carry ads for this type of work. But be careful to deal with a legitimate company. Check it out with the Better Business Bureau before involving yourself.

Ads often appear which tell you that you can make a good living addressing and stuffing envelopes at home. Be skeptical of this, for these days virtually all such work is done by machine. Instead, consider more promising businesses like repair work, tutoring, free-lance writing, copy and proofreading, credit collection service, and income tax preparation, all of which involve little or no capital investment, and customers are seldom hard to find. Free-lance copyreaders and proofreaders are in demand by small publishers, universities, and business firms. Writers doing free-lance work have a wide field. It does not mean only magazine articles and books, but also writing verses for greeting cards and fillers for publications, as well as advertising copy and speeches or reports for businessmen and politicians. Credit collection can easily be conducted from the home by mail or telephone. If you know bridge, knitting, sewing, cooking, or play a musical instrument, tutoring is a possibility. If you are fluent in a second language, establish a translation bureau to work on letters or documents for businesses, or help students and private individuals with correspondence. I know a "retired" professor of chemistry who at 88 keeps very busy translating papers, articles, and books, as well as delivering lectures on chemists' biographies, his specialty.

Lecturing is another possibility. Many clubs or organizations will pay to listen to a description of your former business, your hobby, or your travels, or even how you dealt with common problems, such as, how to raise children, stop smoking, or lose weight. After you have delivered a few lectures and find you like it, you can contact a lecture agent to book a tour for you.

Selling real estate can also be done out of your home. You

will need some training and you must pass a test for a state license before you can be your own boss.

If you own a car and know your way around your community, another way to earn a small income is by showing visitors the local points of interest. Prepare a brochure and leave it in hotel lobbies, bus stations, and railroad terminals.

Or you could offer a shopping service to wealthy or lazy people who know their own taste is not too good. This could be great fun for the woman with an eye for fashion who enjoys shopping and has the stamina for it.

Perhaps you can do research for lawyers, college professors, or authors, or even some private individuals who want family histories and genealogies dug up. If you are a long-time resident of a community, contact your local governing body and offer to work up a file of historical data. The chamber of commerce or other group of businessmen may be willing to support a compilation of local history as a promotion project.

Local businessmen might also be interested in specialized mailing lists. You can easily compile a list of new babies, newlyweds, etc., from local newspapers. Gear your list to a selected market and approach the specific businesses.

Your newspaper offers a wealth of other possibilities. A man in Omaha, Nebraska, had the idea of checking ads to inform supermarkets and banks of the give-aways offered by their competition. His business was so successful that he now has employees checking 200 newspapers for supermarket, retail drug, general merchandise, and department store ads. He remarks, "The information was always available. I just organized it to make it an actionable marketing tool in the hands of my clients." He has 100 clients now, paying between $20,000 and $40,000 per product category a year for weekly reports. He literally found gold in the newspaper ads.

MAIL ORDER BUSINESSES

Another type of enterprise that can be tailored to your capabilities and started with very little capital (a few hundred dollars would do) is the mail order business. Your own basement or spare room could become the center of activity. But an effective operation will entail a good deal of preparation, study, planning, and experimentation until a good selling idea is found. The mail order business is well suited to women as well as men, and while some advanced education is helpful, it is not essential. With determination and sagacity the average person can master the principles of selling by mail. You will need to choose a product, select the right price, and test the pull of your advertising. The local library has books which will help introduce the subject to you and you will find some schools offering instruction in the field. You can also learn a lot about the business just by observing mail-order advertising. Perhaps you can get to know some people in the business in your area. Call and ask them questions; they will probably be very hospitable and tell you what you want to know. The Small Business Administration in Washington, D.C., will send you free on request, "Selling by Mail Order." The prospects in mail-order now are probably better than ever. Small operators net about $3,000 to $5,000 a year, while full-time operators are reported to earn between $40,000 and $50,000.

Many successful mail-order businesses depend on a special skill or knowledge of the owners. But others are based on such standard items as fancy foods, artists' supplies, auto accessories, chemicals, and custom-blended tobacco, perfume, and tea. A startling new invention is not required to build a profitable business. There is an old saying in the trade, "If it can be sold, it can be sold by mail." That gives you an idea of the range of possibilities. Most mail-order businesses that are successful for a long time sell a product that the customer buys again and again, like cigars, uniforms, or office supplies. Select a line you would take pleasure in promoting; things you make yourself are especially good.

Persons qualified in a trade or profession are often able to market their service by mail. Information, instruction, or education by mail is one of the most profitable areas of mail-order selling. Economic advisory services and other current information bulletins are put out by specialists in various fields. Newsletters offer social security information, retirement news, and sermons for ministers. Those familiar with trades such as radio, carpentry, painting, or mechanics, could work up an inexpensive treatise or a series of them to sell. Information on the uses of chemical substances, teaching how to play a musical instrument, or speed typing are other subject possibilities. Bookbinding, photographic work, and commercial art work are some of the services sold by mail. Patent search, advertising writing, and consultations on public relations projects are others. One idea that a retired couple is making pay is selling trading cards. These pictures of baseball and other sports personalities are bought by children and collectors. The business started as a hobby but they are now handling a substantial volume of mail on just a few small ads each year.

7

LOOK TO THE FUTURE

Benjamin Franklin was 81 when he sat in the Constitutional Convention in Philadelphia. At about that time he had his townhouse rebuilt, adding bedrooms and a large new library, something few people venture at his age. Most of us move into less, rather than more, space in our senior years. As Franklin was shelving his books in his new library, a friend came in and Franklin is reported to have explained, "It has always been my maxim to live on as if I was to live always."

Franklin's attitude is worth emulating—to continue to plan, to seek, and hopefully to find throughout one's lifetime. But in past years the norm for the elderly has been to retire to the protective bosom of their children's homes, to cease striving, and to quietly await the end, which often was not long in coming. Today, attitudes are changing. Because they have more years to look forward to, most older persons want to remain independent and active. In the last century, another generation of living, or a period of 20 years, has been added to the average life-span. These added years, plus better health and higher levels of education, have led to needs and desires past generations did not have. Yet society has been slow in recognizing these needs and desires, and opportunities for fulfillment in the senior years are sorely lacking. The elderly themselves must see to it that the necessary changes are made on their behalf, politically, socially, and in the business world.

SENIOR POWER

Other groups, like Blacks, Chicanos, and women, are forcefully demanding new and expanded rights for themselves, and participation in society's decision-making processes. The aged, often termed the fastest growing minority in the nation, must do the same or risk being pushed into what has been described as a "subculture of poverty and social uselessness." Unfortunately, many older persons are turned off by the idea of militancy.

Not so Robert S. of Sacramento, California. At 95, he has been arrested a total of 315 times for picketing in the state Capitol. Considered the dean of the Capitol protestors, he says, "Complaining is the first of your rights and you should preserve it. When you can't complain, you're lost." A former boxer, Methodist minister, and Salvation Army major, Mr. S. has been prowling Capitol corridors with his portable walking chair since 1966, carrying signs denouncing officials and protesting their actions. The public defender during a trial after one of his arrests said, "There's something very, very American about this little old man daring to prick the consciences of people who are very big people."

Like Mr. S., I believe we have a right, and even a duty, to complain and to demand improvement in the situation of older persons. Today there are over 22.3 million persons 65 or older, and another 10 million between 60 and 65. These large numbers represent an even greater proportion of the electorate because of the regular voting habits of older people. According to the Study of Generations, conducted by the University of Southern California, over 90 percent of them are registered, contrasted with 65 percent of the younger adults over 21, and 41 percent of the 18 to 21 age group. Senior citizens can become a power that few politicians will choose to ignore. As one senior citizen said, "Anyone who doesn't understand that people need political organization, doesn't know where it's at." Hobart Jackson, former Chairman of the National Caucus on Black Aged supported this view saying, "If older persons are ever going to get their just entitlement, it will come from efforts in the political process. I don't subscribe to the view that social programs for the elderly are welfare. We're really talking about entitlements, rights, and priorities."

Individuals acting alone can only do so much. It is by

joining together and pooling their efforts that large accomplishments will come. The value of group action is well recognized in our society: businessmen join chambers of commerce, workers join unions, minorities form civil rights organizations. Group action is needed to successfully influence public policy decisions. Yet in the past the elderly have been slow to organize. Only in comparatively recent years have senior citizen organizations sprung up which attempt to deal with the specific needs of their members. In several states well-organized and articulate statewide organizations have mobilized considerable support for improved state programs and services for older people. Two such groups are the California Legislative Council for Older Americans and the Congress of Senior Citizens in Florida. But it is on the national level that the senior citizen groups are becoming most visible. They are questioning "who gets what" to determine whether older persons are getting their fair share and influencing administrative, legislative, and judicial decisions that affect the lives of their members. Following are descriptions of a few of the better known of these national organizations:

GROUPS WORKING FOR THE ELDERLY

The largest is the American Association of Retired Persons (AARP) which, combined with its sister organization the National Retired Teachers Association (NRTA), boasts 7.9 million members and a substantial growth rate monthly. Although separate entities, both organizations share goals and political activities. Any person 55 or older may join AARP and become eligible for an array of services, from adult education courses to income tax counseling. Its address is 1909 K Street, N.W., Washington, D.C. 20049.

The NRTA was founded in 1947 by Dr. Ethel Percy Andrus, a prominent California educator, and its initial goals centered around improving state pensions and federal tax benefits for retired teachers. Soon, Dr. Andrus became disturbed by the frustrations experienced by the elderly in obtaining adequate life and health insurance. In 1956 she successfully obtained affordable group coverage for NRTA members. This innovation attracted the interest of thousands of retirees who were not teachers and led to the formation of the AARP in 1958. During the period of its early growth, the group was concerned primarily with enlarging the range of benefits available to its members—auto insurance, drugs priced within their means; travel service, information brochures, magazines, and others. Since 1967, however, lobbying for senior citizens' rights has been stepped up and now AARP–NRTA is represented by a twelve-man team of lobbyists on Capitol Hill. Its original perspective and social outlook were closely linked to that of business enterprise, especially the insurance industry, but since the early 70s AARP–NRTA has worked to get acceptance in Washington as a non-partisan body. As a result, its voice is now heeded by Democrats and Republicans alike.

Still, the AARP–NRTA has been criticized for being too low-key and for not putting sufficient resources into attacking the problems faced by senior citizens. Its goals, while including a political dimension, have tended to emphasize individual uplift and social betterment. For example, when Medicare was under consideration, AARP–NRTA did not oppose it, but it was not among the bill's active promoters. Currently, however, the group has come out against mandatory retirement and in favor of needed reforms in the social security system.

Still, AARP–NRTA's bias toward the industrial-management viewpoint is implicit in the fact that not a single former labor union official currently sits on the Board of Directors, whereas a number of former businessmen do. In contrast, there is the National Council of Senior Citizens (NCSC) whose leadership is securely in politically aggressive and socially involved industrial union hands. Built around the remnants of the Senior Citizens for Kennedy organization in the 1960 presidential campaign, the NCSC was formed for the sole purpose of lobbying for Medicare. Charles Odell of the United Auto Workers and James C. O'Brien of the United Steel Workers, who ran programs for retired workers in the AFL–CIO, persuaded their unions to put up small amounts of money to lobby for passage of the legislation. The concensus among observers is that NCSC did play a significant role in the approval of Medicare by Congress.

NCSC has since grown in membership and diversity of goals. Currently it consists of over 3,000 affiliated senior citizen clubs, with a total membership of 3.5 million. But actual dues-paying members who contribute directly to NCSC number about 250,000, an increase of over 200 percent since 1971. It has worked to expand its membership base beyond labor union retirees and now includes middle-class and non-union-related people. Yet the larger industrial unions, particularly the auto workers, machinists, steelworkers, electrical workers, and the AFL–CIO Industrial Union Department have been known to generously subsidize the NCSC budget. NCSC offers a wide spectrum of services to its members, including travel, drugs, and legal aid at attractive prices. Politically, NCSC recently went on record as firmly opposing the complete elimination, or undue liberalization, of the Social Security test because they believe that the cost of such action might better be used in other ways, such as increased Social Security payments. The address of the NCSC is 1511 K Street, N.W., Washington, D.C. 20005.

At a time when most of the senior citizen organizations are becoming more aggressive, probably the most militant of all is the Gray Panthers. They have no formal membership, no dues, and no age requirements. They estimate their membership at 2,000, 15 percent of whom are under 65. Ms. Margaret Kuhn, the 68-year-old leader of the Gray Panthers, is a diminutive lady who does not look anything like the stereotype of the radical she is. As she puts it, "We're not mellowed sweet old people. We're outraged, but we're doing something about it." The members of her group have used consciousness-raising seminars and public speaking engagements to make older persons aware of the problems and the discrimination they face. Politically, like the AARP, the Gray Panthers opposes forced retirement and works for an improved health system. But whereas the AARP lobbies for these reforms within the established system, the Gray Panthers believes that the American system itself needs changing. The address of the Gray Panthers is Tabernacle Church, 38th and Chestnut Streets, Philadelphia, Pennsylvania.

Taking Ms. Kuhn's activities as inspiration, the Task Force on Older Women was created in 1973 within the National Organization for Women. Concentrating on discrimination faced by women, the Task Force is working for changes in social security regulations, such as giving credit for housewives' work; on the problems of age discrimination in employment; pension inequities; and the plight of widows. Tackling the physical and mental needs of older women, it emphasizes self-help to counter women's traditional dependency on men. Instructional pamphlets on many subjects important to women are published. The Task Force's address is 434 66th Street, Oakland, California 94609.

ORGANIZE FOR ACTION

I have mentioned only a few of the more than 300 national organizations representing the elderly today. Investigate as many as you can. If they represent what you think, join them. If not, form your own group. But do work together for economic, social, and health-system changes. Improvements will not happen by themselves; some definite and concentrated action will need to be taken.

The following sections highlight actions which are needed to effect improvements in the area of employment opportunities for the elderly.

INCREASE EMPLOYMENT OPPORTUNITIES

Expanded Labor Market. Older workers, like minority groups and women, find more ready acceptance in business and industry when total employment is high. When jobs are scarce, though, these groups are selected out of a share in the "job pie." Not only are older workers at a disadvantage when competing for job vacancies in a tight labor market, but there is also pressure to squeeze them out of jobs they already hold in order to provide work for younger persons.

During the Great Depression, in order to deal with the unemployment problem, Social Security was established to encourage older workers to retire, thus eliminating part of the population from competition for scarce jobs. This is the historical basis for the retirement test. More recently, the New York City administration, as related in Chapter 1, attempted to force retirement of their older civil servants during a budgetary crisis. In bad times, analogous actions are used by private businesses. The International Business Machines Corporation (IBM), for example, which has a tradition of never laying off workers for economic reasons, recently offered special pension inducements to their older workers to effect early retirements.

Since older job seekers benefit from a full employment situation perhaps more than any other group, that should be our national goal. Instead of pitting older workers against younger ones for scarce jobs, we need to aim for a policy of economic expansion and more jobs for all. Certainly we have the brain-power, and we should exhibit the will, to develop a meaningful job for every able person who wants to work. With all that remains to be done to provide a healthy and happy life for all our citizens, there need be no shortage of work opportunities. It is just plain wasteful not to use all the energy and talent available to improve the quality of our lives.

Equal Opportunity for Jobs. While we fight for a greater total number of jobs, we must also work for equality of opportunity for older workers in existing jobs. Some new ways to do this are:

1. A review of federal contracts by the Secretary of Labor to encourage employment of qualified older workers in the same way as is now being done for minorities and women in affirmative action programs. Or the federal Vocational Rehabilitation Act (a 1974 amendment covered all Vietnam veterans) which requires private companies, institutions with government contracts or grants, and all government agencies, to develop major programs to hire handicapped work-

ers, might be used in developing legislation for senior citizens.

2. Create jobs in the public sector and in non-profit agencies through government grants for those elderly, especially the handicapped, who cannot find acceptance in industry. Representative Edward Koch of New York recently introduced legislation for the formation of a senior citizen job corps which would provide 50,000 jobs for persons aged 62 or over with low incomes. Unfortunately the bill did not get beyond the House Education and Labor Committee. Such legislation should be reintroduced, but changed to include middle-income individuals as well as the poor.

3. Provide government training, job counseling, and placement programs specifically for persons over 60, or earmark funds for this group within existing programs. In 1974 a bill to provide job training for the elderly passed the Congress but was vetoed by President Nixon. Efforts are being made to reintroduce it.

4. Transportation is a major factor in finding employment. Since many of the elderly do not own cars, they are particularly handicapped in their job search in suburban and rural areas where mass transit is lacking. Greater federal subsidies and other forms of government action are needed to encourage the development and improvement of public transportation nationwide.

5. To make the skills of the elderly more competitive and update their technical information, continuing education and re-education are needed. More educational facilities geared to their needs, plus special outreach programs to encourage participation, should be established. Many older workers find it strange and difficult to go back to school after many years of work and life. Special efforts are needed to help them return to formal education. New and more effective methods of training adult workers also need to be developed. It has been found for instance, that for the elderly the pace of instruction has to be slowed, or ideally the pace should be under the trainee's control. In addition, learning by doing has yielded better results among the elderly than memorizing

instructions for later use. Zeroing in on the educational problems of the elderly, the 1971 White House Conference on Aging recommended that a Division of Education for Aging be established in the U.S. Office of Education to be responsive to the educational needs of the elderly. To date, it does not exist.

An important side effect of extended adult education pointed out by educators is that it could be a catalyst in changing the attitudes of society by reintroducing the younger generation to the older generation. Increased contact between them might develop respect in the young for the experience and wisdom of the aged, and the aged might better understand the values, ambitions, and complaints of the young.

Compensate Employers for Increased Costs. To aid the employment of the hard-core unemployed, federal programs such as the Work Incentive Program (WIN) offer employers certain tax advantages. Twenty percent of the cash wages of workers hired under WIN, for example, may be claimed by the employer as a federal income tax credit. Similar programs exist to aid the employment of veterans. Why not extend the same advantages to employers who hire the elderly, train them, and otherwise upgrade their skills?

Fringe benefits provided by employers—pensions, group life, accident, and health insurance—assets in most working situations, often operate indirectly to restrict the employment of older workers. Some of the most common current restrictive pension provisions are:

1. Limiting or not crediting service after a stated age, thus encouraging retirement at that age. Sixty-five percent of the workers surveyed by the Bureau of Labor Statistics in 1973 were enrolled in plans which had this feature.

2. Exclusion of newly hired older workers from participation in the pension plan. This effectively hinders the hiring of older persons because employers, concerned about their public image, do not want to have to retire them later without pensions.

3. Restrictions on post-retirement employment in the same industry, or even any gainful work. Forty percent of the plans studied by the Bureau of Labor Statistics had such restrictions, which were most prevalent in the construction, mining, and transportation industries. An analogous provision was discovered by the staff of the Senior Skills Foundation, Inc., when it attempted to interest Sears, Roebuck & Company in employing some individuals over 65. The Sears pension system stipulates that a portion of the benefits made to retirees be considered profit-sharing, and treated as long-term capital gains for income tax purposes under a special IRS provision. The regulation states that should the recipient return to work, the total pension payment becomes subject to the full tax. Sears management uses this provision as a basis for refusing to employ persons over 65. They contend that they cannot re-employ their own former workers over 65, and that therefore they should not take on any others. The Senior Skills Foundation presented Sears with a reinterpretation of the IRS provision which would allow for the re-employment of most retirees without adversely affecting their income tax saving, but it was rejected as unacceptable by the company.

When the Age Discrimination in Employment Act was enacted, one of its stated purposes was to discourage pension provisions of the types described above, but to date this has not been accomplished. I believe additional public pressure is now needed to end discriminatory pension provisions.

Besides pension provisions, the handling of workmen's compensation cases has also created problems. Since many awards have been made lately for pre-existing conditions, employers are becoming reluctant to employ older workers. The answer may be to establish an equalization fund out of which employers could be compensated for the increased costs of all fringe benefits attributable to newly hired older workers. Money for such a fund could be generated by taxing pension plan contributions and health insurance premiums paid by employers and/or employees plus additional funds as needed from the general revenues of the federal government.

Two specific suggestions to counteract higher pension

premiums, which rise sharply with increasing age (older workers are sometimes referred to as "pension liabilities"), are:

1. Make provision for workers to carry earned pension credit with them to new employment.
2. Set up multi-employer plans under which contributions generally are the same for each worker regardless of age.

Social Security Reform. The "retirement test," the Social Security regulation which reduces benefits for workers under 72 whose earnings exceed a specified amount, has been termed the most unpopular and least understood feature of the law. It forces many older persons to evaluate whether the wages from a full-time job, considering the effort involved, warrants foregoing part or all of their Social Security benefits for that year. Of course, some decide to work even if it means sacrificing their Social Security. Statistics show a decrease in the number of persons receiving Social Security payments after having applied for benefits, a decrease attributed to their return to full-time work. One such person is Helen S., who said, "By earning over the maximum I end up only slightly better off than if I had just stayed home and collected. But my job does so much for me socially and psychologically that I don't care." But some retirees do care, so they look only for part-time work, keeping their earnings within the maximum allowed by Social Security. Unfortunately, part-time work is scarce in many fields.

I believe abolition of the retirement test provision is essential for fairness, since only wages are counted for this purpose. Wealthy people whose incomes are derived solely from investments, rents, and similar sources can collect their full Social Security checks each month no matter how high their unearned income. In a number of countries, particularly France and Greece, the old age pension is regarded as an annuity to which the worker is entitled on reaching a certain age, whether or not he has retired. Many prominent people in this country (Barry Goldwater, for one) endorse the annuity idea and have come out against continuation of the retirement test. The American Association of Retired Persons has for several years made the repeal of the earnings limitation a part of their legislative program.

Alternatives to the complete abolition of the retirement test, which could serve as interim actions, are:

1. Lowering of the age at which benefits are no longer denied working recipients. The American Association of Retired Persons has suggested permitting unlimited earnings for those over 70, instead of 72.

2. Permitting persons to receive Social Security benefits with no reduction up to the point where benefits plus earnings equal $5,000 a year.

Other reforms which allow Social Security recipients to keep more of what they earn would be:

—Stop collecting Social Security taxes from the wages of working people over 65.

—Increase benefits for those who retire late above the present one percent annual addition.

—Exempt from income taxes those earnings which equal the amount of benefits a recipient loses because he works.

Extend and Enforce the Age Discrimination in Employment Act (ADEA). Compliance with the ADEA in the past years has been lax. Because of lack of enforcement, the law has not had the desired effect, and discrimination in the labor market is still very much a fact of life. It has been estimated that one out of every two available jobs is closed to persons over 55, and one out of four is closed to persons over 45.

Discrimination is often subtle and disguised to keep within the law. For example, when an older job applicant is told he is "overqualified," chances are the real reason is his age. Or an older worker with fifteen years of experience may be turned down because the job description calls only for "two to four years experience." A high school diploma may be made a requirement, resulting in the rejection of an older applicant with limited formal schooling whose years of experience may however make him the equal of a younger high school graduate. Or, to close out older workers who were educated years ago, the job qualification may specify "recent schooling." Fortunately, at least two courts have already ruled that advertisements for "new grads," "recent college graduates," and "college students" violate the ADEA.

The elderly may also lose out because of a pre-employment physical examination, even though physical fitness may have no relevance to the job. Aptitude tests are also screening out older workers, not because these tests are good predictors of job success, but because they have been standardized on younger people. To judge expected job performance is always a difficult task, but certainly using the recent education and experience of young people as a norm produces tests which are inappropriate for measuring the wisdom of the elderly.

As with job discrimination against women and minority groups, the aged often do not know why they are being turned down. Discrimination is so subtle and difficult to identify, that it requires time-consuming and delicate investigative procedures. Increased funding and staffing are necessary to adequately enforce the ADEA. Improved staffing would also allow for greater policing of the legitimate use of the exceptions in the law. For example, non-compliance is allowed if age is a bona fide occupational qualification, reasonably necessary to the normal operation of a particular business. This is the point on which a suit is pending against the McDonnell Douglas Corporation, challenging its practice of removing pilots from flight status at age 50.

Perhaps the only effective solution to age discrimination against older workers is an all-out campaign to change the stereotyped ideas about the aged held by the public in general and employers in particular; to alter people's attitudes so they will focus on the advantages that come with aging, and not the disabilities; and to help people discard ideas which denigrate the elderly and their place in society. The U.S. Senate Special Committee on Aging has observed that age discrimination is the only form of discrimination that enjoys widespread social approval within corporate life. More people are discriminated against in employment because their hair is white than for any other reason.

Faced with pressure during the 1971 White House Conference on Aging, the President extolled the virtues of the elderly and made promises to ameliorate unacceptable conditions through expanded federal resources and new programs. But so far government action has been of the token variety, such as designating an annual "National Employ the Older Worker Week." Adequate funds have never been designated for the basic educational effort needed to create better understanding. We need to tell and show employers that older workers can compete with younger workers, and actively involve them in programs which allow employers to discover this for themselves. A study of employers who gave physical requirements as their reason for setting age limits on jobs shows that 70 percent had not studied the problem and had no objective basis for their conclusions. There were also vast differences in the specific cut-off age for jobs involving similar duties, ranging from a low of 25 to a high of 60.

The 1971 White House Conference on the Aging recommended extending the ADEA to workers over 65. In order to implement this recommendation, many bills have been introduced in Congress, but with little success. Senator Hiram Fong of Hawaii, sponsoring one such bill, emphasized to the Senate that several studies have clearly demonstrated the value of hiring older workers. "It is imperative that America reexamine its employment and retirement policies, both overt and subtle, to the end that all persons, regardless of age, have a clear right to participate in the productive activities on which our total wealth ultimately depends," he said. The bill was referred to the Senate Labor and Public Welfare Committee and was never heard of again. Ten states currently have no upper age limit in their state laws against discrimination in employment. They generally report satisfaction with this and no undue problems of enforcement. Effort must be made to have the federal law changed correspondingly.

The Case Against Mandatory Retirement. The practice of involuntary or mandatory retirement is a particularly widespread form of age discrimination in employment, affecting at least fifty percent of all workers. Most work in large manufacturing concerns, banks, insurance companies, and utilities of substantial size. And according to the Social Security

Administration, more than three-fifths of those forced into retirement did not want to quit working. In fact three out of every four men would work after 65 if given the opportunity and the financial incentive, and nine out of ten are physically capable of doing so.

Among the aging there are few signs that the work ethic is losing its importance, perhaps because pension incomes are too small and are becoming increasingly smaller with inflation. Based on data from the Social Security Administration, the average retiree receives a sixty percent cut in his previous income upon retirement. At the same time it is found that retirees want to consume as much as they did when they were younger. From a purely financial point of view, the vast majority of people over 65 are just not ready to retire. Denying older persons the right to work withholds from them the opportunity of meeting their economic needs, and forces many to live in poverty for the rest of their days.

I have received many letters from people who are unwilling victims of mandatory retirement rules. Here are two that are typical: A woman wrote, "When I reached 65, the company I was working for as proofreader, production editor, copy editor, and editor, told me there could be no exceptions, regardless of skills, health, good attendance, and the need for my services. My immediate supervisor and his department head both asked to have me continue working, and I made a direct appeal to the company president—all to no avail because of the 'rule.'" And a professor at the University of Pennsylvania wrote, "I am 64 and according to the rules of my university, next year, when 65, I ought to retire. And I *do not want to!* I am healthy, full of vigor, my teaching performance is much better than average, I publish a lot (in fact more than the average). I have small children, 10 and 12, and have not reached the apex of my career. Do you have any practical advice?" I replied that some individuals in similar situations have sued.

In recent years efforts have been made to strike down mandatory retirement rules by court action but with inconclusive results. Cases currently pending have behind them the theory that the right to work is a fundamental constitutional guarantee which cannot be abridged or curtailed through the application of arbitrary standards. The retirement policy which selects a given age and conclusively presumes that the individual is non-productive upon attaining that age is inconsistent with reality. It has yet to be shown that those who wish to remain at work are typically least productive. One study of 1,500 men aged 65 in 31 companies revealed that of those who wanted to continue their regular jobs after 65 (64 percent of the total), two-thirds were considered acceptable for continued employment by their employers.

Many talented and able individuals are lost to our productive facilities by rigid retirement rules. Recognition of this has induced some companies to waive retirement regulations for selected employees, usually persons working on the professional or administrative level. Employment after 65 is not uncommon at this level, and it is estimated that about 56 percent of all persons with professional training and experience are still employed after 65. Also not subject to mandatory retirement rules are many self-employed craftsmen whose skills and talents would have been lost to society had they not continued to work after 65. Andrew G. at 85 is still manufacturing a unique precision gauge in Rockland County, New York. In production since 1911, the instrument is calibrated to test the accuracy of measurements to the ten-thousandth of an inch. Without a sales force, solely on the reputation of the product, orders continue to come in from all over the world. Still alert and wiry, Andy handles all the work single-handedly.

Robert C. of Troy, New York, at 75 is keeping alive the rare old seamen's craft of fender knitting. Knitted fenders are the protective coverings used on the bows, sterns, and sides of barges and harbor tugs. Mr. C. says, "Knitting a fender is not an easy task; it requires a lot of skill and some muscle power."

Joseph C. of Spring Valley, New York, at 87 frail and somewhat hesitant of step, is still producing flawless briar pipes of extraordinary beauty. The pipes are sold in the smoke shop owned by his daughter and son-in-law.

Richard N. has been hand-building equipment for fire truck

chassis since the late 1950s. Now 68 and employing only part-time help, he turns out one fire truck every five years. Working with pride and affection on his latest product in a cluttered, dank old building in Cincinnati, Ohio, he remarked, "It takes a while. I'm old-fashioned, I guess. In the old days we all had pride in our work."

Louis I., who at 94 is called the "grand old man" of cut glass and engraving, has been at his craft for more than seventy years. Now his son William, 61, runs the family business in Flemington, New Jersey. But Louis is still seen by visitors to the shop, sitting behind his cutting wheel eight to ten hours a day, smoking a cigar, and enjoying their admiration. He cuts the designs freehand from the 4,500 patterns he has committed to memory. For his 90th birthday he produced 300 eight-inch plates of cut glass, each signed and numbered and of a different design. They were snapped up by collectors all over the world, the orders coming from as far away as South Africa and Australia. "Pop's quite a guy," says his son. "Knowledgeable people regard him as the finest stone-wheel engraver in this century, and certainly one of the most prolific."

As these gentlemen continue to produce, so do many others in the arts, politics, law, and medicine, where professionals are free to carry on according to their individual wishes. Our society accepts them as exceptions to the rule of mandatory retirement so readily applied in industry, though there is no evidence that professionals perform better in their senior years than office or blue collar workers.

One person who took advantage of being in the right field was the actor Robert Young, who returned to his acting career after having tested retirement for six years. In a recent newspaper interview he observed, "How many other fields are there like acting in which you can keep on working when you're 90?" He vividly recalled the vacuity of life in the retirement community. "I tried to live the life of a country squire, and filled my days with pseudo activities. I was marking time on a treadmill. There were some of the unhappiest men in that retirement community," he says. "Former executives, some who had ruled business empires. I'll never forget the day one of them complained, 'I woke up this morning and thought, What in the hell do I do today?'" Robert Young is more fortunate. He is an actor and there was an active career for him to return to when he chose. He cannot get over how much he has changed as a result of returning to work. "I astound myself," he says, "I zing around the sound stage or jump on a plane to do a benefit, or handle a thousand other activities. I've never had such vitality before."

Others have experienced similar improvement in health on returning to work. While it is difficult to show conclusively that physical or emotional illness can be caused directly by denial of employment opportunity, physicians who treat older persons often recognize that many physical ailments are the result of inactivity and the lack of a meaningful and productive life. The older person who has lost the satisfaction and confidence that come with performing useful work can easily fall prey to loneliness and depression, which in turn can produce or accelerate symptoms of illness. Loss of status, lack of purposeful activity, and the fear of becoming dependent and isolated all affect the physical and mental health of the unwillingly retired. It is for these reasons that the American Medical Association believes that for the very old, those over 70, retirement may be more psychologically damaging than for those younger.

I have a poignant letter from a concerned daughter who wrote, "I hope you and your organization can help me. I know this sounds dramatic, but my father's life is at stake. My father has had a long and illustrious career in public administration in Texas—over 30 years. For 20 years he was the City Manager of one of the fastest growing cities in the state. He "retired" to take a year off to travel. When he came back, he was hoping to find some employment but found that his "connections" were in retirement also. He has made several attempts to find work but after 30 years in public service he doesn't know anything about how to find a job. Money isn't so important, being useful *is*. He and my mother are back sitting on a Greek island now. I know he feels that there is nothing left for him but to grow old and die, although he is only in his early 60s and very healthy. I know someplace there must be an employer who could make use of his fantastic talents (about 15 years ago he was labeled one of the top 10 city managers in the country), but I sure don't know how to find it. I'd be very grateful if you could give me some suggestions to help bring this great man back to life!" I hope my book will give direction to this man and the thousands more like him.

While individuals suffer from forced retirement, society does, too, for the unemployment and underemployment of older workers is not without cost. Increases in the proportion of nonworkers to workers places an ever greater burden on those who remain in the work force. In a recently released study conducted by the National Council on Aging, an overwhelming majority of Americans of all ages said that government has a duty to provide for older persons at a level which allows them to live comfortably no matter how much they earned during their working years. An admirable consensus, but who will pay for it? Eighty-one percent of those surveyed indicated that general tax revenues should be used. In other words, the money will come from those who work. For regardless of whether retirement income is in the form of social security, public assistance, or private insurance, the fundamental economic fact is that a proportion of the national output consumed in any particular year by the retired is being produced by the working population. The young pay for the old. It has been estimated that for every 100 persons of working age there are 18.2 who are 65 or older. This ratio will increase with advances in life expectancy. And as more and more people reach retirement age, the load on society of unproductive people will become more and more burdensome.

Additional hospital space and nursing homes are maintained to care for those dependent elderly who fall apart, to a great extent, because society expects them to. Taxpayers' dollars can be saved by keeping older persons independent, and out of institutions and off welfare rolls. The remarks of one elderly welfare recipient saddens me: "When we were kids, we was told to work hard. I used to work 12 to 14 hours a day all my life. Now they kicked me out 'cause I'm too old. I could work, but now I'm just a leech taking welfare. I got no choice—I gotta eat. I feel so low."

Employers, however, cling to the practice of mandatory retirement, giving usually these two reasons: First, it provides them with a tactful way to remove older workers and advance younger ones. Second, the mandatory retirement rule relieves them of the responsibility of making decisions on an individual basis, of singling out one worker for continued employment after 65, and another for retirement at that age.

We certainly need to open up places for younger workers, but not at the expense of older workers. To take jobs from the elderly solely for this reason is to admit that our society cannot effectively utilize the talents, skills, and abilities of a large number of its citizens. Such waste should be unacceptable and we should aim to have our economy develop to the level at which it can absorb all who are able and willing to work. Yet in bad times, when the economy is particularly hard hit, there is increasing pressure to force retirement at an ever lower age, despite the hardships this creates. A letter that recently appeared in *The New York Times* is illuminating on this point. "Last month, when I read that New York City proposed to retire employees earlier than had been anticipated in order to retain younger people, I thought it an eminently fair idea. Then I was retired by my employer, with all due consideration, and, indeed, with generosity—but still retired. As this is written, I have been retired exactly two days, and a whole new vista of boredom and frustration has opened up before me. I now understand that retiring people before they are psychologically prepared for it can be a most wrenching experience for them. My wife, who works, has been kind enough to assure me that I have not yet become a vegetable, but she holds out no guarantee for next week. . . . I suppose I will adjust in time, but for the sake of others who may or may not be able to do so, perhaps the city should think twice before urging retirement on employees who may not be fully aware of all the implications."

This man retired with a "generous" pension. But for others, early retirement at 55 or 60 brings with it reduced pension benefits, and of course less Social Security. Such lowered income could produce real hardships when inflation adds its effect. However, even unions are endorsing and pressing for early retirement in order to open up additional jobs, claiming that the setting of the "normal" retirement age at 65 is a myth.

Sixty-five as the retirement age is believed to have been chosen arbitrarily when Chancellor Bismarck established the forerunner of all national retirement systems almost one hundred years ago in Germany. Of course, at that time not many people reached that age and even fewer survived for very long after. In the United States in the early 1900s, although retirement ages were fixed at 70 or 75 in many companies and industries, the framers of the Social Security Act took 65 as the age of eligibility based on Bismarck's decision. Since then, pressures have continued to lower the retirement age even though more people are living longer, with improved health, mental ability, capability, and potential. According to a study of the Banker's Trust Company of New York, 90 percent of all major labor contracts covering 7.8 million workers already provide for retirement before age 65 under some circumstances. Furthermore, over one million workers are subject to forced early retirement at the discretion of their employers. Unfortunately, as early retirement becomes more common, the age at which employers will be hiring older workers for new jobs and vacancies will be pushed downward.

The second reason given for the use of chronological age for retirement purposes, that it obviates the task of evaluating individual job performance, raises a question that needs the attention of our industrial psychologists. A sounder approach to the problem has to be sought. We know that chronological age alone is a poor indicator of working ability, for the working performance of some persons warrants their retirement at 25, while others should be kept on till 95 or older. Studies show that health, mental and physical capacities, work attitudes, and overall job performance are individual traits at any age. The range of differences of these factors increases with age, so much so that perhaps the greatest differences of all in the ability to perform on the job are among the elderly. Ideally, therefore, the older person should be evaluated as an individual on the question of his continued employability. Ralph Waldo Emerson said, "A man's years should not be counted, until he has nothing else to count."

New techniques for dealing with people as individuals need to be developed to assist employers. Clearly no one should remain in a position if he or she cannot meet its demands, but neither should a competent employee be forced to quit or retire simply because of reaching a certain age. Such judgments should be made on the basis of facts, not blanket assumptions. One method might be the use of physical examinations.

Recently, this procedure was used to resolve a complaint registered in New Mexico under that state's age discrimination law, which covers workers of all ages. The complaint concerned an employee of a company operating at the Holloman Air Force Base, who was forced to retire at 65 under the company's long-standing mandatory retirement program. A conciliation agreement was worked out whereby the emloyee would submit to a physical examination by a doctor to ascertain his physical fitness to perform his duties, and an examination would be administered each succeeding year if his employment continued. The company further agreed to institute a voluntary retirement program for all employees reaching 65, based on a similar arrangement. In concurring in the agreement, the complaining employee remarked, "Whatever each individual's circumstances are pertaining to retirement, I believe he should have the freedom of choice, and as word gets around, more people will come to making the matter of retirement discretionary and not mandatory." The New Mexico Human Rights Commission, which negotiated the agreement, took appreciative note of the company's resolution of the complaint, saying, "Such an attitude is exemplary in a time when far too many employers encourage the aging process by forcing retirement on employees before they have reached the point in their lives where they are no longer productive."

Even for those elderly who have physical limitations,

provision can be made for continued employment. The poor health that afflicts some elderly really dictates only the kind of work they might perform and does not warrant the conclusion that they are unemployable. A study by a number of medical practitioners who examined all their male patients of 60 to 69 revealed that 74.4 percent were considered fit for their original employment; 11.6 percent were unfit for their original employment but fit for other work; and only 14 percent were unfit for any employment.

Aging is clearly more significant for some occupations than for others. Most of us are unsuited either physically or psychologically for many jobs. It is difficult to find even a few people who are physically suited to pilot planes, work on docks, tend blast furnaces, or stand up under heavy construction work. People who cannot do these things are physically handicapped in relation to these jobs, but most are certainly capable of doing other work.

Some sophisticated techniques for measuring an older worker's physical, and sometimes emotional, fitness for continued employment have been developed. The techniques go beyond the already well-developed tests for assessing skills and measuring the ability to perform specific tasks. One measure pioneered by the Canadian Government is called the GULHEMP scale, which is an acronym formed from the initial letters of the seven areas measured: General physique, Upper extremities, Lower extremities, Hearing, Eyesight, Mentality, Personality. The Gulhemp scale measures a worker's abilities, and the results are then compared with a chart showing the minimum abilities required for different jobs. The technique has been used for many years in the Canadian Department of Veterans Affairs and by a prominent aircraft company in Toronto. In 1970 an experimental project was set up at the Industrial Health Counseling Service (IHCS) in Portland, Maine, using the Gulhemp scale. Almost 100 Portland industries have subscribed to IHCS, and more than 1,000 middle-aged and older workers who had been unable to find work because of their age have found jobs after being Gulhemped, demonstrating clearly that capacity and ability, not chronological age, are the determining factors in job performance. Prospective employers who consider certain job applicants "too old" for particular types of jobs tend to change their minds when confronted with Gulhemp results. Raymond W., a soft-spoken and intense man of 63, had a varied working background ranging from president of a lumber company to office worker and night watchman. He suffered a heart attack in the last occupation and when he recovered, he fruitlessly sought work. "Company after company turned me down. It was my age, though many just said I was overqualified." Referred to Gulhemp, the test results indicated his continued ability to work, and shortly thereafter he had no trouble obtaining a job as an office clerk for a manufacturer of building materials.

Efforts are underway to export the Gulhemp program to other states and communities for the method has shown that the great majority of persons with some limitations have remaining capacities which can be gainfully utilized. One enthusiastic supporter of the program observes, "Age is never a barrier to working, only physical limitations are. And these can be measured and fully compensated for by using the yardstick called Gulhemp." The problem then becomes one of proper placement, or if no appropriate job vacancy exists, some job restructuring may be warranted.

The technique of job restructuring can be effectively utilized to help employ the elderly. Tasks too difficult for most elderly, because of strength or speed requirements, for example, could be removed, and only those activities they are capable of performing put together into new job assignments. Such job redesign can be accomplished in almost any occupational field, for most jobs as they currently exist constitute groupings of tasks that were put together purely as a result of circumstances, not out of studied need. If job tasks were to be reëxamined and then grouped together in such a way as to fit the abilities of different workers, better utilization of our total manpower resource would result and all would benefit, employer, employee, and society. Only when all members of society can function to the limit of their capabilities is society strong, forceful, and stable, according to John Dewey, noted American philosopher.

Some form of job restructuring could be used to create the many more part-time jobs so often desired by retirees. The restructuring technique has had wide acceptance in the Scandinavian countries of Denmark, Norway, and Sweden, where jobs have generally been adapted to the various ages, and never call for undue exertion on the part of any worker. In those countries there are many elderly who never need to retire. Unfortunately, in our country there has been considerably more emphasis on preparing people for retirement than on altering jobs to make them suitable for older workers.

Resolution of the problem of forced retirement at a specific age might come about as an indirect benefit of an approach to life that is gaining favor nationally, particularly among young people. Based on the conviction that rigid lifetime patterns of work and leisure need complete rethinking, this approach calls for a meshing and intertwining of the currently distinct stages of schooling in adolescence, work in maturity, and retirement in old age. Concern with widespread worker dissatisfaction and apathy has focused the attention of both employers and unions on such a possible mingling of education, work, and leisure. Edgar Faure, economist and former Prime Minister of France, has criticized our three "immutable" categories of life—"when people study but do not work, . . . work and do not study at all, and finally . . . [are] supposed neither to work nor to study." Gosta Rehn, the Director of Manpower and Social Affairs of the Organization of Economic Cooperation and Development, an international agency for economic planning based in Paris, has proposed an integrated system of periods of work and periods of study and leisure, adding the imaginative idea of a free transfer of income from one's work to support one's study and leisure time, even an advance credit to cover costs of early education. The efforts of these men in attacking the work and retirement patterns that have characterized our past are fueled by a determination that they not be automatically extended into the future.

But until such drastic changes in lifestyle are accomplished facts, interim solutions need to be effected. One idea with which a small group of companies and government agencies have been experimenting is trial-and-gradual-retirement programs designed to ease the "retirement shock" in the transition from full-time work to full-time leisure, a time often beset by problems, particularly when the change is abrupt and involuntary. To be suddenly flung from the active to inactive category, to be classified as old, and to undergo a severe drop in income and standard of living can have serious psychological and spiritual consequences. An extreme case was reported of a worker who on the eve of his retirement could not leave his desk at the end of the day and had to be sedated to be removed from the building. He was literally frozen with fear. Even tough individuals suffer. As one robust truck driver put it, "All of a sudden I was part of nothing and I felt unwanted. I cried like a baby. There's nothing worse than to be turned out into the world like that. It's terribly lonely, very difficult for the mind to adjust to."

Experience has shown that if there is an easing into retirement at a pace more in keeping with the wishes of individual employees, the physical and psychological disturbances so often associated with any sharp change can be minimized. I recall Oliver Wendell Holmes' words: "The riders in a race do not stop short when they reach the goal. There is a little finishing canter before coming to a standstill." The trial or gradual retirement programs basically accomplish this. By reducing the work time of employees as they near retirement, the programs permit them to experience some added leisure time and affords them an opportunity to explore tentative retirement plans. It can be used to investigate new places to live, or to further one's education in preparation for a post-retirement job or engrossing hobby. Sometimes its value is in allowing a gradual adjustment to a decreased income.

While details differ among plans, in general the gradual retirement procedure is that an employee approaching normal retirement age (sometimes a year or two earlier, sometimes less) is given the option of a shortened work year through additional vacation time, or a reduced work week entailing part-day or part-week scheduling. Where a day off each week is involved, Friday or Monday is usually chosen, based on the belief that the three day weekend would help the employee adjust to more leisure time. The age at which such reduction may start and whether full wages are paid vary with the employer involved.

Some gradual retirement plans operate after the normal retirement age has been reached. In these, the reduced time is customarily not paid for, so these programs are more accurately described as semi-retirement plans. The Wm. Wrigley, Jr., Company, of Chicago, uses such a plan. Employees physically able to continue to work after the normal retirement age of 65 are allowed to do so, but they must take one month of leave without pay during the first year, two months during the second year, and so on. Wrigley's management reports that the program is going very well, attributing its success to "the aspect which allows each employee to choose how fast he is to give up active employment."

Job-sharing for about a year with one's successor is another variation which gradually relieves the job pressures on the soon-to-be-retired, as the successor takes over more and more of the responsibilities. Along these lines, some gradual retirement plans call for transfer to less demanding duties. Such a phase-out retirement program is offered by the General Services Administration of the federal government, where key staff members may elect reassignment from high tension positions to advisory or specialized jobs, usually at a lower level, but at no reduction in salary. Management thus has the opportunity to replace retiring workers prior to actual retirement so there is continuity in the position through having the predecessor available to coach his successor. In some cases, the program is also available to lower level employees. Older workers who are experiencing poor health welcome this opportunity to reduce their job tensions, but others use it simply to prepare themselves for a more sedentary retirement lifestyle. Departmental regulations at the General Services Administration are careful to emphasize that an employee must apply for participation in the program on his own initiative and that it may not be used as a force-out method. Of course, compulsion in such action would be in violation of the federal Age Discrimination in Employment Act. In early 1975, a law suit on this particular point was decided in favor of an abused employee. The case was brought against the Exxon Corporation by the estate of a research chemist who, after nearly 30 years of employment, had been assigned to menial tasks when he refused to retire voluntarily at age 60. The award of $750,000 ordered by the jury was the highest ever granted under the law up to that time.

Besides gradual retirement plans, trial retirement programs are also offered in a number of the agencies of the federal government. In these programs, an employee eligible for early retirement may elect to retire for a year with the option of returning at the end of that time if he so wishes. In other words, this option is available to employees considering early retirement but who are concerned about "unknowns" such as finances, living arrangements, and activities, and who are uneasy about taking an irrevocable step. The trial retirement allows time to experiment with launching a new career, exploring the desirability of living in another region, and generally offers the reluctant retiree a taste of more leisure time. About 10 percent of all those eligible have elected this option and the reports are that about 10 percent of them return to work. Occasionally someone asks to return to work briefly but at a different location. When possible, the request is honored, but for some agencies the problem of providing appropriate re-employment and the difficulty of filling the vacated position on a temporary basis only have presented serious problems. For this reason, and because of mandated reductions in staff during the 1975 recession, many agencies have found it increasingly difficult to fulfill their commitments in a satisfactory manner to their "trial" retirees, and a number have chosen to discontinue the program.

So there is some experimentation going on to alter rigid retirement rules. Those programs being tried deserve our support, at the same time that we call for faster and more decisive changes. The abolition of mandatory retirement rules will come, but only when the elderly organize and demand it. They must be allowed to decide for themselves whether to work or not. Freedom of choice is the essential ingredient.

Meanwhile, for those already involuntarily retired, get back to work! Do yourself a favor; go out and find the job you want and help keep yourself healthier and happier. I wish I could reach out and take the hand of each of you and firmly assure you that there is so much you still can do. In the words of Tennyson, "Tho' much is taken, much abides. . . . How dull it is to pause, to make an end, to rust unburnish'd, not to shine in use! As tho' to breathe were life!"

APPENDIX A

STATE OFFICES ON THE AGING

In 1965 only 21 state governments had departments of the aging. Today all 50 states have such offices, including three which have cabinet level status—Massachusetts, Connecticut, and Illinois. These agencies serve as advocates for older citizens, coordinate activities on their behalf and provide information about services and programs. In addition to the state offices for the aging listed below, area agencies have been created within states. Many cities also have established departments on aging in their local governments. The name and address of the nearest local agency on aging may be obtained from your state agency.

On the national level, the government agencies on aging are the Federal Council on Aging, the Administration on Aging, the Senate Special Committee on Aging, and recently a comparable House committee. The Senate Special Committee on Aging, established in 1961, has been very useful in identifying and studying the special needs and problems of the aging, and making recommendations to the Senate on appropriate legislation. The committee is divided into seven subcommittees studying consumer problems; employment and retirement income; federal-state-community services; health; housing; long-term care; and retirement. For information in any of these areas, simply address your inquiry to the Senate Special Committee on Aging at Washington, D.C. 20510.

STATE OFFICES ON THE AGING

Alabama Commission on Aging, 740 Madison Ave., Montgomery 36104, Tel. (205) 269–8171

Alaska Office on Aging, Dept. of Health & Social Services, Pouch H, Juneau 99801, Tel. (907) 586–6153

Arizona Bureau on Aging, Dept. of Economic Security, 543. E. McDowell, Rm. 217, Phoenix 85004, Tel. (602) 271–4446

Arkansas Office on Aging, P.O. Box 2179, Hendrix Hall, 4313 West Markham, Little Rock 72203, Tel. (501) 371–2441

146 [Help Yourself to a Job

California Office on Aging, Health & Welfare Agency, 455 Capitol Mall, Suite 500, Sacramento 95814, Tel. (916) 322-3887
Colorado Division of Services for the Aging, Dept. of Social Services, 1575 Sherman St., Denver 80203, Tel. (303) 892-2651
Connecticut Department of Aging, 90 Washington Street, Room 312, Hartford 06115, Tel. (203) 566-2480
Delaware Division of Aging, Dept. of Health & Social Services, 2413 Lancaster Ave., Wilmington 19805, Tel. (302) 571-3482
District of Columbia Office of Services to the Aged, Dept. of Human Resources, 1329 E St., N.W. (Munsey Bldg.) Washington 20004, Tel. (202) 638-2406
Florida Program Office of Aging & Adult Services, Dept. of Health & Rehabilitation Services, 1323 Winewood Blvd., Tallahassee 32301, Tel. (904) 488-4794
Georgia Office of Aging, Dept. of Human Resources, 618 Ponce de Leon Ave., Atlanta 30308, Tel. (404) 894-5333
Hawaii Commission on Aging, 1149 Bethel St., Room 311, Honolulu 96813
Idaho Office on Aging, Dept. of Special Services, Capitol Annex No. 7, 509 N. 5th St., Room 100, Boise 83720, Tel. (208) 384-3833
Illinois Department on Aging, 2401 W. Jefferson St., Springfield 62706, Tel. (217) 782-5773
Indiana Commission on the Aging and the Aged, Graphic Arts Bldg., 215 N. Senate Ave., Indianapolis 46202, Tel. (317) 633-5948
Iowa Commission on the Aging, 415 W. 10th St. (Jewett Bldg.), Des Moines 50319, Tel. (515) 281-5187
Kansas Services for the Aging Sector, Div. of Social Services, Social & Rehabilitation Services Dept., State Office Bldg., Topeka 66612, Tel. (913) 296-3959
Kentucky Aging Program Unit, Dept. for Human Resources, 403 Wapping St., Frankfort 40601, Tel. (502) 564-6930
Louisiana Bureau of Aging Service, Div. of Human Resources, Health & Social Rehabilitation Services Admin., P.O. Box 44282, Capitol Station, Baton Rouge 70804, Tel. (504) 389-6713
Maine Bureau of Maine's Elderly, Dept. of Health & Welfare, State House, Augusta 04330, Tel. (207) 622-6171 or 289-2561
Maryland Commission on Aging, State Office Bldg., 1123 N. Eutaw St., Baltimore 21201, Tel. (301) 383-2100
Massachusetts Department of Elder Affairs, 120 Boylston St., Boston 02109, Tel. (617) 727-7751
Michigan Offices of Services to the Aging, 3500 N. Logan St., Lansing 48913, Tel. (517) 373-8230
Minnesota Governor's Citizens' Council on Aging, Suite 204, Metro Square Bldg., 7th and Robert Sts., St. Paul 55101, Tel. (612) 296-2544

Mississippi Council on Aging, P.O. Box 5136, Fondren Station, 510 George St., Jackson 39216, Tel. (601) 354–6590

Missouri Office on Aging, Div. of Special Services, Dept. of Social Services, Broadway State Office Bldg., Jefferson City 65101, Tel. (314) 751–2075

Montana Aging Services Bureau, Dept. of Social and Rehabilitative Services, P.O. Box 1723, Helena 59601, Tel. (406) 449–3124

Nebraska Commission on Aging, State House Station 94784, 300 S. 17th St., Lincoln 68509, Tel. (402) 471–2307

Nevada Division of Aging, Dept. of Human Resources, Kinkead Bldg., Rm. 101, 505 E. King St., Carson City 89701, Tel. (702) 885–4210

New Hampshire Council on Aging, P.O. Box 786, 14 Depot St., Concord 03301, Tel. (603) 271–2751

New Jersey Office on Aging, Dept. of Community Affairs, P.O. Box 2768, 363 W. State St., Trenton 08625, Tel. (609) 292–3765

New Mexico State Commission on Aging, Villagra Bldg., 408 Galisteo St., Santa Fe 87501, Tel. (505) 827–5258

New York Office for the Aging, N.Y. State Executive Dept., 855 Central Ave., Albany 12206, Tel. (518) 457–7321

North Carolina Governor's Coordinating Council on Aging, Administration Bldg., 213 Hillsborough St., Raleigh 27603, Tel. (919) 829–3983

North Dakota Aging Services, Social Services Board, State Capitol Bldg., Bismarck 58501, Tel. (701) 224–2577

Ohio Commission on Aging, 34 N. High St., Columbus 43215, Tel. (614) 466–5500

Oklahoma Special Unit of Aging, Dept. of Institutions, Social and Rehabilitation Services, Box 25352, Capitol Station, Sequoyah Memorial Bldg., Oklahoma City 73125, Tel. (405) 521–2281

Oregon Program on Aging, Human Resources Dept., 315 Public Service Bldg., Salem 97310, Tel. (503) 378–4728

Pennsylvania Office for the Aging, Dept. of Public Welfare, 510 House & Welfare Bldg., P.O. Box 2675, Harrisburg 17120, Tel. (717) 787–5350

Rhode Island Division on Aging, Dept. of Community Affairs, 150 Washington St., Providence 02903, Tel. (401) 528–1000 or 277–2858

South Carolina Commission on Aging, 915 Main St., Columbia 29201, Tel. (803) 758–2576

South Dakota Program on Aging, Dept. of Social Services, State Office Bldg., Illinois St., Pierre 57501, Tel. (605) 224–3656

Tennessee Commission on Aging, S & P Bldg., Room 102, 306 Gay St., Nashville 37201, Tel. (615) 741–2056

Texas Governor's Committee on Aging, Southwest Tower, 8 Fl., 211 E. 7th St., Austin 78711, Tel. (512) 475–2717

Utah Division of Aging, Dept. of Social Services 345 S. 6th E., Salt Lake City 84102, Tel. (801) 533-6422

Vermont Office on Aging, Dept. of Human Services, 81 River St., Montpelier 05602, Tel. (802) 828-3471

Virginia Office on Aging, Suite 950, 830 E. Main St., Richmond 23219, Tel. (804) 786-7894

Washington Office on Aging, Dept. of Social & Health Services, M.S. 43-3, Olympia 98504, Tel. (206) 753-2502

West Virginia Commission on Aging, State Capitol, Room 420-26, 1800 Washington St., E., Charleston 25305, Tel. (304) 348-3317

Wisconsin Division on Aging, Dept. of Health & Social Services, State Office Bldg., Room 686, 1 W. Wilson St., Madison 53702, Tel. (608) 266-2536

Wyoming Aging Services, Dept. of Health & Social Services, Div. of Public Assistance & Social Services, Hathaway Bldg., Cheyenne 82002, Tel. (307) 777-7561

APPENDIX B
SENIOR CITIZEN EMPLOYMENT SERVICES

Arizona

Glendale, Plus 60 Personnel, Inc., 5850 W. Northview, Tel. (602) 939-5698
Phoenix, Plus 60 Personnel, Inc., 1029 N. First St., Tel. (602) 258-7787
Retirement Achievements, 1439 N. First St., Tel. (602) 253-8934
Scottsdale, Plus 60 Personnel, Inc., 7700 E. Roosevelt, Tel. (602) 994-2330

California

Hemet, Experience, Inc., 26951 Cawston Ave., Tel. (714) 658-8710
Los Altos, Retirement Jobs, Inc., 730-C Distel Dr., Tel. (415) 964-4881
Los Gatos, Retirement Jobs, Inc., Main & Tait Sts., Tel. (408) 354-5171
Palo Alto, Retirement Jobs, Inc., 514 Bryant St., Tel. (415) 326-6180
San Francisco, Retirement Jobs, Inc., 225 Kearny St., Tel. (415) 781-4831
San Jose, Retirement Jobs, Inc., 211 S. First St., Montgomery Apts., Tel. (408) 294-3558
Eastside Office: 50 S. King Rd., Tel. (408) 251-3003
Southside Office: 5585 Coltie Rd., Tel. (408) 578-2925
San Mateo, Retirement Jobs, Inc., 126 W. 25th Ave., Tel. (415) 574-4474
San Rafael, Marin Senior Coordinating Council, Inc., The Whistlestop, 930 Tamalpais Ave., Tel. (415) 456-9062
Stockton, Senior Manpower Program, 135 W. Fremont St., Tel. (209) 466-0944

Colorado

Denver, Older Americans, Inc., 3100 Cherry Creek S. Dr., Tel. (303) 722-7890

Connecticut

New Haven, W.H.E.E.E.—"We Help Elders Establish Employment," 53 Wall St., Tel. (203) 777-5317
Norwalk, Senior Personnel Placement Bureau, Inc., Frost Bldg., Room 218, 520 West Ave., Tel. (203) 838-7553
Stamford, Senior Employment Service, Inc., 1642 Bedford St., Room 107, Tel. (203) 327-4422 or 327-5716
Windsor, Department of Social Services, Town Hall, Tel. (203) 688-3675

Delaware

Wilmington, Employment Services for Older Delawareans, Wilmington Senior Center, Inc., 1901 N. Market St., Tel. (302) 654-4441

Florida

Clearwater, Senior Citizens Services, Inc., 940 Court St., Tel. (305) 442-8104
Fort Lauderdale, Project for the Elderly, Broward Community College, 3501 S.W. Davie Rd. and 225 E. Las Olas Blvd., Tel. (305) 792-7130
Hallandale, Project for the Elderly, Broward Community College, Austin-Hepburn Center, 8th Ave. and Foster Rd., Tel. (305) 792-7130
Miami, Project Elderly's Oasis—The Older Adult Serving in Society, Miami-Dade Community College, Downtown Campus, 300 N.E. Second Ave., Tel. (305) 577-6705
Miami Beach, South Beach Activities Center, Workmen's Circle Bldg., 25 Washington Ave., Tel. (305) 673-6060
Oakland Park, Project for the Elderly, Broward Community College, Collins Recreation Center, 3900 N.E. 3rd Ave., Tel. (305) 792-7130
Pompano Beach, Project for the Elderly, Broward Community College, North Campus, 1000 Coconut Creek Blvd., Tel. (305) 792-7130
St. Petersburg, Senior Citizens Guidance & Referral Service, Mirror Lake Adult Center, 709 Mirror Lake Drive, Tel. (813) 821-4593

Georgia

Atlanta, Golden Age Employment Service, 793 Piedmont Ave. N.E., Tel. (404) 875–9443 or 876–4482 or 874–1969

Hawaii

Wailuku, Added Income Program, Maui County Commission on Aging, 200 S. High St., Tel. (808) 244–7837

Idaho

Boise, Retirement Jobs of Idaho, Inc., 700 Robbins Rd., Tel. (208) 342–3605

Illinois

Chicago, Jewish Vocational Service, 1 S. Franklin St., Tel. (312) 346–6700

Harvey, South Suburban Council on Aging, Operation TASK—Temporary Assignment for Senior Knowledge, 156 E. 154th St., Tel. (213) 596–3001

Urbana, S.T.E.P.—Senior Talent Employment Pool, Older Workers Program, 1303 N. Cunningham Rd., Tel. (217) 384–3768

Indiana

Indianapolis, Senior Enterprises, Inc., Employment Opportunities, 2 W. Vermont St., Tel. (317) 634–7007

South Bend, REAL Services, 622 N. Michigan, P.O. Box 1835, Tel. (219) 233–8205

Maine

Waterville, Senior Citizens' Employment Service, 10 Center St., Tel. (207) 872–5838

Maryland

Baltimore, Over-60 Employment Counseling Service of Maryland, Inc., 309 N. Charles St., Tel. (301) 752–7876

Chevy Chase, Over–60 Counseling and Employment Service, 4700 Norwood Dr., Tel. (301) 652–8072 or 652–8073

152 [Help Yourself to a Job

Massachusetts

Brookline, Project RETAIN, Jobs for Senior Citizens, 83 Centre St., Tel. (617) 734-9116

Michigan

Muskegon, Senior Power, Senior Services of Muskegon, Inc., 304 Monroe Ave., Tel. (616) 722-2019

Missouri

St. Charles, Project Earn, Jewish Employment & Vocational Service, 205 S. Main St., Tel. (314) 724-9092
St. Louis, Project Earn, Jewish Employment & Vocational Service, 1727 Locust St., Tel. (314) 241-3464
University City, Project Earn, Jewish Employment & Vocational Service, 701 West-Gate, Tel. (314) 725-0130

Nevada

Las Vegas, Senior Citizens Employment Service, Nevada Catholic Welfare Bureau, Inc., 820 Las Vegas Blvd. S., Tel. (702) 382-2042
Reno, Senior Employment Service, Nevada Catholic Welfare Bureau, Inc., 275 E. 4th St., P.O. Box 5415, Tel. (702) 329-6644

New Jersey

East Orange, The Jewish Vocational Service Work Center on Aging, 67 N. Clinton St., Tel. (201) 674-2415
Hackensack, SPR'Y, Senior Personnel Registry, 133 River St., Tel. (201) 342-2200 or 489-SPRY
Montclair, Senior Citizens Placement Bureau, Young Women's Christian Association, Montclair-North Essex, 159 Glenridge Ave., Tel. (201) 746-8360 or 746-5400
Summit, SAGE/OWL, Older Workers Lifeline, 50 DeForest Ave., Tel. (201) 273-5554

New York

Albertson, New Life Institute, Human Resources Center, Searingtown Road, Tel. (516) 747-5400, Ext. 332

Binghamton, GROW (Gaining Resources for Older Workers), Action for Older Persons, Inc., c/o N.Y. State Employment Service, 40 Main St., Tel. (607) 772-8770
New Rochelle, Senior Personnel Placement Bureau, Inc., 22 Church St., Tel. (914) 235-7725
New York City, Federation Employment & Guidance Service, 215 Park Ave., S., Tel. (212) 777-4900
>   Path, Federation of the Handicapped, 154 W. 14th St., Tel. (212) 242-9050 (Services only for low income applicants.)
Nyack, 60-Plus, 10 N. Broadway, Tel. (914) 358-9391
Rego Park, Queens Job Center for Older Adults, Federation Employment and Guidance Service, 97-29 64th Rd., Tel. (212) 275-6700
Syracuse, Action Coalition to Create Opportunities for Retirement with Dignity, Inc. (ACCORD), 264 E. Onondaga St., Tel. (315) 422-2331 or
>   Civic Center, 13 Floor, 421 Montgomery St., Tel. (315) 425-3436 or 425-3427
West Nyack, Senior Skills Foundation, Inc., P.O. Box 76, Tel. (914) 358-3442
White Plains, Senior Personnel Employment Committee, Fairview Greenburgh Community Center, 32 Manhattan Ave., Tel. (914) 682-5258
>   Senior Personnel Employment Committee, Inc., 158 Westchester Ave., Tel. (914) 761-2150

Ohio

Cleveland, Skills Available, 1001 Huron Rd., Tel. (216) 781-2944
Columbus, Senior Citizens Placement Bureau of Franklin County, 880 East Broad St., Tel. (614) 252-5238

Oregon

Eugene, H-E-L-P, Help Elderly Locate Positions, 673 W. 10th St., Tel. (503) 343-7816
Medford, Comprehensive Program for Older Persons, Rogue Valley Council on Aging, 510 E. Main St., Tel. (503) 779-6691

Tennessee

Chattanooga, Senior Employment Service, Inc., 10th & Newby Sts., Tel. (615) 756-5950

154 [Help Yourself to a Job

Texas

San Antonio, Senior Citizens Employment Service, 307 Marshall St., Tel. (512) 222-1294

Utah

Salt Lake City, Opportunity Center, Ability Agencies, Inc., 252 S. 5th E., P.O. Box 11611, Tel. (801) 532-2942

Virginia

Alexandria, Senior Citizens Employment and Services of Alexandria, Inc., 121 N. Asaph St., Tel. (703) 836-4414
Arlington, Senior Adult Counseling and Employment Service, Arlington County Dept. of Personnel, 2100 N. 14th St., Room 116-118, Tel. (703) 558-2589

Washington

Edmonds, Senior Employment Service, South County Senior Center, Inc., 220 Railroad Ave., Tel. (206) 774-5555
Everett, Senior Employment Service, Senior Services of Snohomish County, 3402 112th S.W., Tel. (206) 355-1112 or 745-1112
Spokane, Senior Workers Service, Employment Security Dept., W. 300 Mission Ave., Tel. (509) 456-2734

Wisconsin

Milwaukee, Seniors Offer Services, Educational and Vocational Guidance Institute, Jewish Vocational Service, 1360 N. Prospect Ave., Tel. (414) 271-3844 or
Beth Am Center, 5418 W. Burleigh St., Tel. (414) 445-4014

INDEX

ACTION programs: 39–40
Adult education: 33–34
Age: and confidence, 64–65; discrimination, 19, 21, 127–128; and esteem, 6; handling questions about, 77–78, 91; and letters of application, 69; mental fitness and, 7, 138–139; myths about, 7–12; physical activity and, 6, 9–12, 138; in other societies, 6; stereotypes, 128; studies, 6–7
Age Discrimination in Employment Act (ADEA): 19, 21–22, 51, 125; extending and enforcing, 127–129, 143
Agricultural cork: 41–43
Aides, in community services: 43–44, 60
American Association of Retired Persons (AARP): 43, 118–120
Anxiety: interviews, 75; returning to school, 37
Application forms: 74–75
Application letters: 69–73
Arts and crafts: 110

Boredom: 4, 132
Business: see Office work

Child care work: 28, 36, 39, 42
Civil Service employment: 48–49
College programs: 34–35, 42

Community programs: see Local programs
Commuting: 66
Companion jobs: 28, 60
Compulsory retirement: 2, 8, 18, 129–144
Consulting work: 99–102
Cottage industry: 110–113

Decision-making, reasons to work: 1–7, 130, 133
Department of Labor programs: 40–44; listings of, 45
Discrimination: by employers, 19, 21; within the law, 127–128

Economics: inflation, 2; recession businesses, 87–90
Education: adult, 33–34; background appraisal, 30–32, 127; at colleges, 34–35, 42; under federal government, 32; home-study courses, 36; programs available, 32–37
Elderly: attributes of, 9, 12–13; employability of, 44; firms that hire, 94–96; preference for, 13
Emergency Employment: 46
Employers: compensating them for increased costs, 124–126; discrimination by, 19, 21, 129; and mandatory retirement, 135; what they look for, 12–13

155

Employment opportunity, increasing: abolishing mandatory retirement, 129–144; compensating employers for increased costs, 124–126; equal opportunity for jobs, 122–124; expanded labor market, 121–122; extending and enforcing ADEA, 127–129; reforming Social Security, 126–127

Employment services: commercial, 51–52; for elderly, 52–63; jobs handled, 56; names and addresses of, 149–154; nonprofit, 52–62; other services performed by, 59–62; procedures, 54–55; state, 50–51; U.S., 50–51

Equal opportunity for jobs, 122–124

Experience: 12, 64

Factory jobs: 29

Federal government programs: 32–33; ACTION, 39–40; civil service system, 48–49; Department of Labor, 40–44; employment services, 50–51; income requirements, 38; listings of, 45; for retired military, 47, 99; where to find, 38

Financial need: 1–4, 130

Fitness, measuring: 138–139

Former occupation, and job selection: 23, 57–58

Foster Grandparent Program: 39–40

Franchise operations: 108–110

Future planning: groups working for elderly, 118–121; increasing employment opportunities, 121–144; and inflation, 2–3; senior power, 116–117

Gray Panthers: 120–121
Green Light: 40, 42–43
Green Thumb: 40, 41–42
Guard services: 27, 89–90
GULHEMP scale: 138–139

Health: measuring fitness, 138–139; returning to work and, 6–7, 132–133
Health care work: 89
Hobbies: 23, 88
Home-study courses: 36

Income: and eligibility for government programs, 38, 39; median, 3; pensions, 3, 125, 135–136; retirement, 3; and Social Security, 13–19, 126; unemployment insurance, 18–19, 125
Industrial work: 27, 31, 94
Insurance field: 97–98
Interviews: age question, 77–78; follow-up to, 79–81; obtaining by letter, 69; obtaining by phone, 68; preparing for, 29, 73–76; other questions, 78–79; using resumés, 82

Job banks: 50–51
Job counselors: 31, 57
Job hunting: age question, 77–78; commuting considerations, 66; follow-ups, 79–81; in hard times, 87–115; interviewing, 73–79; letters of application, 69–73, 80–81; personal contacts, 63–64; phone techniques, 68–69; preparing a re-

sumé, 82–86; sources of employment, 45, 65; using want ads effectively, 66–68
Job performance: 8–12
Job restructuring: 139–140
JOBS: 32
Job selection: educational needs, 30–37; in employment agencies, 56–57; former occupation, 23, 57–58; listings and state locations, 45; for physically disabled, 109; problems for women, 28–29; self-analysis, 29–30; for unskilled retirees, 25–27; using old skills in a new way, 24

Laws: age discrimination, 19–20, 21–22, 51, 125, 127–129, 143; knowledge and application of, 22; minimum wage, 19–21; state vs. federal, 21
Lecturing: 111
Legislative intern: 46
Letters: of application, 69–73; follow-up, 79–81
Local programs: 47–48

Mail order businesses: 113–115
Medicare: 16
Mental ability: 7, 138–139
Military, retired: 47, 99
Minimum wage: 19–21
Myths, about aging: 7–12

National organizations: for women, 121; working for the elderly, 118–121; working for increased employment opportunities, 121–144
National Retired Teachers Association (NRTA): 43, 118–120

Office work: 28, 32
Older Americans Act: 7

Part-time work: 43–44, 61, 92–94, 126; job restructuring and, 140
Pensions: 3, 125, 135–136
Personal contacts: 63–64
Personnel departments: 70
Phone techniques: following up interviews, 79–80; requesting interviews, 68–69
Physical activity: 6, 9–12, 138
Physical examination: 128–129, 137, 138–139
Physically disabled: 109
Poverty: 2–3
Professional fields: consulting work, 99–102; teaching, 98–99
Public Employment Program (PEP): 32
Public Service Careers Program (PSC): 32
Public service work: 43

Real estate: 96–97, 112–113
Recession businesses: 87–90
Reference books: 30, 70, 73
Referrals: 81
Repair services: 87
Resort job market: 93–94
Resumés: 69, 82–86
Retail sales work: 27, 93
Retirement: boredom in, 4, 132; case against, 129–144; chronological age and, 136; easing into, 141–143; employers' view, 135; in hard times, 135; job-sharing, 142–143; mandatory, 2, 8, 18, 129–144; of self-employed, 131; shock of, 141; trial programs, 143–144; voluntary, 19

158 [Index

Retirement test, in Social Security: 14–15, 126

Safety records: 9
Salary: 78
Savings: 3
School, returning to: 37. *See also* Education
Self-analysis: educational background, 30–32; skills, 23, 28, 29–30
Self-employment: and retirement, 131; and Social Security, 14–18, 104–108
Self-esteem: 4–5
Selling occupations: 95–98
Semi-skilled retirees: 25–29
Senility: *see* Mental ability
Senior Aides: 40, 43
Senior Community Service Project: 40, 43–44
Senior Companion Program: 40
Service industries: 93
Sheltered workshops: 102–103
Skilled trades: 102
Skills: analyzing, 23, 28, 29–30; learning new, 32; needed in hard times, 90–92; training in, 33–34; using in a new way, 24–26
Social motivation, for working: 4–6, 133
Social Security: effect on other payments, 18–19; how working increases, 17–18; reforming, 126–127; reliance on, 3; reporting income to, 17; retirement test, 14, 126; rules, 13–19, 92; which earnings count, 16–17
Standard of living, maintaining: 2, 3

State employment services: 50–51
State offices on the aging: 145–148
State regulations: 20–21
Studies, on aging: 6, 7
Supplementary security payments: 18

Teaching: 98–99
Training programs: 33; through employment agencies, 59–60

Unemployment insurance, eligibility for: 18–19
Unions: 119–120
Unskilled retirees: 25–29

Voluntary retirement: 19
Volunteer jobs: 53

Want ads: 66–68
Women: jobs suited to, 27, 97; national organizations for, 121; special problems of, 28–29
Work: in American society, 5; financial need to, 1–4, 130; and life span, 6–7, 133; in other societies, 6–7; psychological reasons for, 4–6, 133; social reasons for, 4–6, 133; and Social Security, 17–18
Work experience, in job selecting: 23
Work Incentive Program (WIN): 124
Workmen's compensation: 125
Work performance, and age: 8–12, 136–137